LET THERE

BE

A CHANGE

TIMOTHY ATUNNISE

TSA SOLUTION PUBLISHING
ATLANTA, GEORGIA

LET THERE BE A CHANGE

Copyright © 2012 by Timothy Atunnise

Unless otherwise specified, all Scripture quotations in this book are from The Holy Bible, King James Version. KJV is Public domain in the United States printed in 1987.

Timothy Atunnise
GLOVIM PUBLICATIONS
Global Vision Ministries Inc.
1096 Bethsaida Road
Riverdale, GA 30296 USA.
info@glovimonline.org
www.glovimonline.org

TSA Solution Publishing
A division of Timat Store, LLC.
Atlanta, GA 30294
timatstore@yahoo.com

Cover Design: Tim Atunnise

ISBN: 978-1477490358

Printed in the United States of America

DEDICATION

This book is dedicated to my wonderful spiritual daughters, Funto Onabokun and Titilola Sogunro, who spent their valuable time to type, proofread and edited the manuscript of this book and made the availability possible at the time promised.
You are precious! May the Lord continue to increase you in wisdom, and in every knowledge in the name of Jesus Christ.

To all intercessors across the globe, the battle is won by the Blood of Jesus Christ.

To my Lord Jesus Christ:
Thank you for the mercy and grace you extend to someone like me.

IMPORTANT NOTICE

Deliverance is a benefit of the Kingdom, only for the children of God. If you have not accepted Jesus Christ as your personal Lord and Savior, this is the best time to do so.

Before you continue, you need to be sure you are in right standing with God if you want to exercise the authority and power in the name of Jesus Christ. The Bible says,

"Then he called his twelve disciples together, and gave them power and authority over all devils, and to cure diseases." - Luke 9:1.

"And these signs shall follow them that believe; in my name shall they cast out devils; they shall speak with new tongues; they shall take up serpents; and if they drink any deadly thing, it shall not hurt them; they shall lay hands on the sick, and they shall recover." – Mark 16:17-18.

These are promises for the Children of God, not just for everyone. Why don't you give your life to Christ today and you will have access to the same promises. Food that is meant for the children will not be given to the dogs.

"But he answered and said, it is not meet to take the children's bread, and cast it to dogs" – Matthew 15:26.

If you really want to be delivered from any bondage of the wicked and be set free from any form of captivity, I ask you today to give your life to Christ. If you are ready, say this prayer with all your heart:

"Dear Heavenly Father, You have called me to Yourself in the name of Your dear Son Jesus Christ. I realize that Jesus Christ is the only Way, the Truth, and the Life. I acknowledge to You that I am a sinner. I believe that Your only begotten Son Jesus Christ shed His precious blood on the cross, died for my sins, and rose again on the third day. I am truly sorry for the deeds which I have committed against You, and therefore, I am willing to repent (turn away from my sins). Have mercy on me, a sinner. Cleanse me, and forgive me of my sins.

I truly desire to serve You, Lord Jesus. Starting from now, I pray that You would help me to hear Your still small voice. Lord, I desire to be led by Your Holy Spirit so I can faithfully follow You and obey all of Your commandments. I ask You for the strength to love You more than anything else so I won't fall back into my old ways. I also ask You to bring genuine believers into my life who will encourage me to live for You and help me stay accountable.

Jesus, I am truly grateful for Your grace which has led me to repentance and has saved me from my sins. By the indwelling of Your Holy Spirit, I now have the power to overcome all sin which before so easily entangled me. Lord Jesus, please transform my life so that I may bring glory and honor to You alone and not to myself.

Right now I confess Jesus Christ as the Lord of my life. With my heart, I believe that God the Father raised His Son Jesus Christ from the dead. This very moment I acknowledge that Jesus Christ is my Savior and according to His Word, right now I am born again. Thank You Jesus, for coming into my life and hearing my prayer. I ask all of this in the name of my Lord and Savior, Jesus Christ. Amen".

I hereby congratulate and welcome you into the Kingdom. You hereby have full access to the benefits, promises and blessings of the Kingdom.

This book is loaded with blessings; you will not be disappointed as you continue to enjoy the goodness of the Lord.

INSTRUCTIONS: HOW TO USE THIS BOOK

If you are new to this method of prayer, please follow this instruction carefully:

Step 1:

Spend enough time in praising and worshiping God, not just for what He is about to do or what He has done, but WHO HE IS.

Step 2:

Unforgiveness will surely hinder your prayer, take time to remember all those who have done you wrong, and forgive them from the bottom of your heart. THIS IS VERY IMPORTANT BECAUSE YOUR DELIVERANCE DEPENDS ON IT.

Step 3:

Believe in your heart that God will answer your prayer when you call upon Him, and do not doubt in your heart.

Step 4:

Pray in the name of Jesus Christ alone.

Step 5:

Repeat each prayer point 25 to 30 times or until you are convinced that you have received answers before you go to the next prayer point. Example: When you take prayer point number 1, you say this prayer over and over again, 25 – 30 times or until you are convinced that you have an answer before you go to prayer point number 2.

Step 6:

It will be more effective if you can fast along with your prayer. If you want total deliverance from your bondage, take 3 days of sacrifice in fasting as you say your prayer aggressively, asking your situation to receive permanent solution and your deliverance will be made perfect in the name of Jesus Christ. Amen!

Table of Contents

THE MEANING OF PRAYER

What is prayer? Prayer is our direct line with heaven. Prayer is a communication process that allows us to talk to God! He wants us to communicate with Him, like a person-to-person phone call. Cell phones and other devices have become a necessity to some people in today's society. We have blue tooth devices, blackberries, and talking computers! These are means of communication that allow two or more people to interact, discuss, and respond to one another. For too many people, prayer seems complicated, but it is simply talking to God.

Prayer is the practice of the presence of God. It is the place where pride is abandoned, hope is lifted, and supplication is made. Prayer is the place of admitting our need, of adopting humility, and claiming dependence upon God. Prayer is the needful practice of the Christian. Prayer is the exercise of faith and hope. Prayer is the privilege of touching the heart of the Father through the Son of God, Jesus our Lord.

The Bible speaks much of prayer. But, sometimes, too often, we ignore prayer and seek to accomplish in the strength of our own will those things that we desire to have or happen. For those of us who are too often guilty of this, we need to bow our knees, confess our sin, receive God's forgiveness, and beg that the will of the Lord be done above our own. God is sovereign and loving and He knows what is best for us and others, even if it doesn't always seem to make the most sense.

We so often come to the Lord with legitimate requests for healing, conversions, and needs and yet the answers we hope for often do not come. We wonder and sometimes doubt. Yet, we persevere and praise God. We pray because we know that God hears us and because we desire to see results. We should pray by faith, trusting God. We should pray consistently, trusting God. We should pray for healing, trusting God. We should pray for others, trusting God. We should pray and when our prayers are answered or are not answered remember this: If we knew what the Lord knew, we wouldn't change a thing.

Prayer changes the one praying because in prayer, you are in the presence of God as you lay before Him your complete self in confession and dependence. There is nothing to hide when in quiet supplication we are reaching into the deepest part of ourselves and admitting our needs and failures. In so doing, our hearts are quieted and pride is stripped and we enjoy the presence of God. James 4:8 says, *"Draw near to God and He will draw near to you."*

I am reminded of another benefit of prayer: peace. *"Be anxious for nothing, but in everything by prayer and supplication with thanksgiving let your requests be made known to God. And the peace of God, which surpasses all comprehension, shall guard your hearts and your minds in Christ Jesus."* - Philippians 4:6-7.

I suppose that we can test our prayer life and dependence upon God by the peace or lack of peace in our hearts. In all things we are to seek the Lord and in His continued presence peace will surely be our gain.

Prayer is the practice of the presence of God.

THE GENESIS

On February 19th, 1988, something remarkable happened; I met the Lord and He gave me a new life.

I was born and raised in Islam, had some study about the religion and was a proud son of my father until my eyes opened and I saw the light. I didn't have the freedom to serve the Lord like other people because my family couldn't know that I gave my life to Christ. I could only attend all night prayer services when everyone in the house was asleep and I snuck back into the house before they woke up in the morning. In the midst of this struggle, the grace of God continued to abound upon me and the relationship with the Lord continued to grow.

After two year of this exciting relationship, I received a calling from the King of kings and the Lord of lords into the ministry to be His mouthpiece; as the Scripture says, "*And we know that all things work together for good to them that love God, to them who are the called according to his purpose. For whom he did foreknow, he did predestinate to be conformed to the image of his Son, that he might be the firstborn among many brethren. Moreover whom he did predestinate, them he also called: and whom he called, them he also justified, them he also glorified*" Romans 8:28-30, this scripture came alive to me because it was in alignment with the revelation that came at this time. It was very elating and apprehensive, how was I to tell my father that I will soon become a pastor because that's what God wanted me to do? I concealed the matter and cast it unto the Lord according to the Scripture, "*Casting all your care upon him; for he careth for you*" - 1 Peter 5:7.

THE CALL

It all happened during a 4-day Easter Retreat at the headquarters of our church, it was a wonderful time in God's presence, the teachings were awe-inspiring, the teachers were outstanding with an incredible knowledge of the subject, the theme of the seminar was "The Coming of Jesus Christ". The atmosphere was filled with love and charged by the fire of the Holy Ghost as in the day of Pentecost; I found myself in the realm where David the Psalmist was when he wrote "......and I will dwell in the house of the Lord forever" - Psalm 23:6. The experience was beyond explanation, it was incredibly marvelous that I wanted it to last forever, it was like heaven.

At the end of the first day, I went over what I learned and couldn't wait for the second day to start. At exactly 1:30am on Thursday April 12, 1990, the Lord woke me up from sleep and started a 5hour long conversation in which he explained my purpose in life, there was a long argument and at the end the Lord made plain that I only have a week to decide to do His will else He will prove to me that He is God. During this week, the Lord uncovered many things; it was shockingly surprise when the Lord told me that my father was called to do the work of God in 1954 and refused because of religion and fear of men, as a result of this the Lord promised that He will have all his male children do the work instead. I later asked my father and he confirmed that he was afraid of what his family and friends will say.

I was privilege to have ample time to do lots of questioning and raising concern in many area of ministry; I encourage anyone called to the ministry today to spend reasonable time with the

Lord asking for direction on the journey you about to begin. In the process of questioning and querying, the Lord made many promises, gave assurance and most importantly entered into covenant with me, many of which have been fulfilled and many are yet to be fulfilled. But the Ancient of Days, the King of kings and the Lord of lords, the Lord our maker has been proving Himself day after day, time after time as a covenant keeping God,

"And said, O Lord God of Israel, there is no God like thee in the heaven, nor in the earth; which keepers covenant, and sheweth mercy unto thy servants, that walk before thee with all their hearts" - 2 Chronicles 6:14

"Know therefore that the Lord thy God, he is God, the faithful God, which keepers covenant and mercy with them that love him and keep his commandment to a thousand generation" - Deuteronomy 7:9

"My mercy will I keep for him for evermore, and my covenant shall stand fast with him" - Psalm 89:28.

One part of the covenant was that whenever I remind the Lord of this particular covenant, "WHATSOEVER" I ask He will do it; this is how the Lord began to teach me about prayer. Does that mean our God is a forgetful God? No. But it is written in the book of Isaiah 43:26, *"Put me in remembrance: let us plead together: declare thou, that thou mayest be justified"*.

THE MANTLE OF PRAYER

Our God is not a forgetful God but He still demands that you open your mouth and ask. He knows your needs and He is able, willing and ready to meet all your needs but the main requirement is that you open your mouth and present your needs before Him in prayer and supplication.

Few months after my ministerial debut, I was assigned to head the deliverance department of our ministry, I was petrified because I had witnessed many unimaginable cases and situations brought to this department. How under heaven would I do this? I asked myself. Tout de suite, Just follow me, the Lord said; and the mantle of prayer was released upon me. This was the turning point in my prayer life. The Scripture says, "*If ye shall ask anything in my name, I will do it*" - John 14:14. Since then, I have witnessed lives being transformed, the sick being healed, sinners being saved, bondages broken, the captives delivered, stubborn mountains removed, situations changed for the better, troubled homes restored and many more, all through the power of prayer.

When people pray,
- The mighty hands of God come down
- Heaven responds as in the days of Elijah
- Situation turns around for good
- Life transforms
- Atmosphere changes and brings favor
- Yokes break
- Burden is removed
- Miracles, signs and wonders follow

- Testimonies follow
- And God is glorified.

If we can just take time to pray, prayer changes things. The Scriptures says, "*Ask, and it shall be given you; seek, and ye shall find; knock, and it shall be opened unto you*" - Matthew 7:7.

During His earthly ministry, the Lord of lords was coming out of Jericho with His disciples and a great multitude; with the virtue to heal and deliver, with an immeasurable anointing upon Him, with the power to transform and to save, with the anointing to rescue and restore, with an overflowing anointing at work to raise the dead, to restore the eyes of the blind, to set free those in captivity and bondage of the devil.

Surprisingly, no one among those that came out of Jericho with Him noticed the virtue at work in Him but Bartimaeus the blind, who has been patiently waiting all his life for this moment. When he discovered that the Lord Jesus came to town, he cried out and plead for mercy, he refused to be hindered, stopped or contained but cried aloud until his cry got the Lord's attention. What can I do for you? Jesus asked. That I may receive my sight! Bartimaeus answered, and the virtue of healing was released, "*Thy faith hath made thee whole*". - Mark 10:46-52. This is a perfect example of great and mighty things that can be done if we can just pray. It is written in the book Jeremiah 33:3, "*Call unto me, and I will answer thee, and shew thee great and mighty things, which thou knowest not*".

EFFECTIVENESS OF PRAYER

"Confess your faults one to another, and pray for one another, that ye may be healed. The effectual fervent prayer of a righteous man availeth much" - James 5:16.

For our prayers to be effective, we must develop a right attitude and an intimate relationship with God.

I have heard many people say repeatedly that God doesn't or wouldn't talk to them. Some believe it's because of their sins or past mistakes and failures; some believe they are unworthy to hear from the King of kings and Lord of lords. Some have great concern in recognizing the voice of the Living God when He speaks. The truth of the matter is it's all about relationship.

Let's assume you are in a foreign land where you don't have any of your relatives or family, and suddenly you hear the voice of one of your closest relatives at the back of the window in the middle of the night, will you recognize the voice? Yes of course! You may answer. Why is that? Because you know the person intimately, and have a good relationship. If you have hard time recognizing the voice of your heavenly Father, you need to examine your relationship with Him, ask yourself, do I really know this God?

For our prayers to be effective, we must have faith in God and trust Him wholeheartedly.

"But without faith it is impossible to please him: for he that cometh to God must believe that he is, and that he is a rewarder

of them that diligently seek him." – Hebrews 11:6

When you pray, you have to believe that the Ancient of Days will answer your prayers. You must be full of expectation and be persistent in your prayer.

"And it shall come to pass, that before they call, I will answer; and while they are yet speaking, I will hear." - Isaiah 65:24

How many of us would like to have a prayer life that gets this kind of results? How many of us even believe that we can have this kind of a prayer life?

We can become more effective in our prayer life. God, through His Word promises us that we can be effective in our prayer lives. Through the Prophet Elijah's example, James shows us that we can all have an effective prayer life.

"Confess your faults one to another, and pray one for another, that ye may be healed. The effectual fervent prayer of a righteous man availeth much. Elias was a man subject to like passions as we are, and he prayed earnestly that it might not rain: and it rained not on the earth by the space of three years and six months. And he prayed again, and the heaven gave rain, and the earth brought forth her fruit." - James 5:16-18

Elijah prayed and there was a drought; he prayed again and rain came. This is a solemn reminder to us that prayer is not simply asking God for the pleasant things we desire, but an earnest yearning for, and entering into, the will of God, for ourselves and others, be it sweet or bitter. Such was the prayer of the Lord in Gethsemane.

"And he went forward a little, and fell on the ground, and prayed that, if it were possible, the hour might pass from him. And he

said, Abba, Father, all things are possible unto thee; take away this cup from me: nevertheless not what I will, but what thou wilt." - Mark 14:35-36

Jesus gives His disciples a lesson on prayer when He cursed the fig tree in Mark chapter 11. He gives four main ingredients to effective prayer.

Elements of Effective Prayer.

"And on the morrow, when they were come from Bethany, he was hungry: And seeing a fig tree afar off having leaves, he came, if haply he might find any thing thereon: and when he came to it, he found nothing but leaves; for the time of figs was not yet. And Jesus answered and said unto it, No man eat fruit of thee hereafter for ever. And his disciples heard it". - Mark 11:12-14

"And in the morning, as they passed by, they saw the fig tree dried up from the roots. And Peter calling to remembrance saith unto him, Master, behold, the fig tree which thou cursedst is withered away. And Jesus answering saith unto them, Have faith in God. For verily I say unto you, That whosoever shall say unto this mountain, Be thou removed, and be thou cast into the sea; and shall not doubt in his heart, but shall believe that those things which he saith shall come to pass; he shall have whatsoever he saith. Therefore I say unto you, What things soever ye desire, when ye pray, believe that ye receive them, and ye shall have them. And when ye stand praying, forgive, if ye have ought against any: that your Father also which is in heaven may forgive you your trespasses. But if ye do not forgive, neither will your Father which is in heaven forgive your trespasses." - Mark 11:20-26

This parable is designed to illustrate to each one of us one great point, our need for faith in prayer. Because believing prayer, taps God's power to accomplish the humanly impossible.

"And Jesus looking upon them saith, With men it is impossible, but not with God: for with God all things are possible." - Mark 10:27

Jesus exhorted His disciples to believe that they have already received whatever they request in prayer. Faith accepts it as good as done even though the actual answer is still future. Have faith in God. That is the key to answered prayer.

There are four key elements to effectual prayer found in these verses.

"Therefore I say unto you, What things soever ye desire, when ye pray, believe that ye receive them, and ye shall have them. And when ye stand praying, forgive, if ye have ought against any: that your Father also which is in heaven may forgive you your trespasses." - Mark 11:24-25

1. Desire or ask when you pray

    Desire is the starting point. The word "desire" means to ask, beg, crave, call for, desire, or require. We get something from God when we have a heart-felt desire to have it. He wants us to have our desires. *"Delight thyself also in the LORD: and he shall give thee the desires of thine heart."* - Psalms 37:4. You might ask, "What if I want something not good?" If you can't pray about it, you shouldn't want it.

    "For he satisfieth the longing soul, and filleth the hungry soul with goodness." - Psalms 107:9

"The fear of the wicked, it shall come upon him: but the desire of the righteous shall be granted." - Proverbs 10:24

"And whatsoever we ask, we receive of him, because we keep his commandments, and do those things that are pleasing in his sight." - 1 John 3:22

"And this is the confidence that we have in him, that, if we ask any thing according to his will, he heareth us: And if we know that he hear us, whatsoever we ask, we know that we have the petitions that we desired of him." - 1 John 5:14-15

2.   Believe When You Pray.

"Jesus said unto him, If thou canst believe, all things are possible to him that believeth. And straightway the father of the child cried out, and said with tears, Lord, I believe; help thou mine unbelief." - Mark 9:23-24. The word "believe" here means: to think to be true; to be persuaded of; to credit, place confidence in of the thing believed; to credit, have confidence in a moral or religious reference; used in the N.T. of the conviction and trust to which a man is impelled by a certain inner and higher prerogative and law of soul; to trust in Jesus or God as able to aid either in obtaining or in doing something: mere acknowledgment of some fact or event.

True belief in God will often be exhibited by continually going back to God for something; it will show that you believe He can do it and that you believe He will do it.

"Ask, and it shall be given you; seek, and ye shall find; knock, and it shall be opened unto you." - Matthew 7:7

3. Receive When You Pray.

    "And Jesus said unto him, Receive thy sight: thy faith hath saved thee." - Luke 18:42
    Receive means to take with the hand, lay hold of, any person or thing in order to use it; to take up a thing to be carried; to take in order to carry away.

    "Now faith is the substance of things hoped for, the evidence of things not seen." - Hebrews 11:1

4. Forgive When You Pray.

    "In this manner, therefore, pray.... forgive us our debts, as we forgive our debtors." - Matthew 6:9-12. We must always keep in mind the importance of asking the father to not only forgive us of our sins, but also to forgive those who have sinned against us.

Jesus has promised to answer our prayers on the recognized premise that petitions must be in harmony with God's will. This enables faith to receive the answers God gives. God is always ready to respond to obedient believers' prayers, and they can petition Him knowing that no situation is impossible for Him.

As you pray the prayer points in this book, believe with all your heart that your prayers will produce the desired results.

SPEAK TO YOUR DAY

Passages To Read Before You Pray:
Psalms 19, 1, 115, 138, Habakkuk 1:5, Isaiah 41:15-20, Joel
2:21-24, Jeremiah 33:14

PRAYER POINTS

1. O God my Father, I thank you for sparing my life to see a brand new day.
2. O God my Father, I thank you for giving me the gift of life.
3. O God my Father, I thank you for giving me another chance to do things right in every area of my life.
4. O God my Father, I thank you for great and mighty things that you are doing in my life, I will forever be grateful.
5. Today O Lord, I confess my sins and errors before you, have mercy upon me, forgive me and cleanse me in the blood of Jesus Christ.
6. I hereby cover myself in the precious blood of Jesus Christ.
7. I am well protected and secured in the Lord, in the name of Jesus Christ.
8. No evil shall come near me and my household today in the name of Jesus Christ.
9. As I am going out today, I will receive favor from man and woman, in the name of Jesus Christ.
10. As I am going out today, I will receive favor from old and young people, in the name of Jesus Christ.

11. As I am going out today, I will receive favor from the people that I know and those that I don't know, in the name of Jesus Christ.

12. It is written that day speaks, I command this day to speak favor to every area of my life, in the name of Jesus Christ.

13. It is written that day speaks, I command this day to speak solution to every situation in my life, in the name of Jesus Christ.

14. It is written that day speaks, I command this day to speak promotion into every area of my life, in the name of Jesus Christ.

15. It is written that day speaks, I command this day to speak success into everything that I lay my hands on today, in the name of Jesus Christ.

16. It is written that day speaks, I command this day to speak breakthrough to all my efforts today, in the name of Jesus Christ.

17. It is written that day speaks, I command this day to speak greatness into my life, in the name of Jesus Christ.

18. It is written that day speaks, I command this day to speak progress into that area of my life that is stagnated, in the name of Jesus Christ.

19. As I am going out today O Lord, let my day be filled with joy and gladness, in the name of Jesus Christ.

20. As I am going out today O Lord, let my day be filled with testimonies in the name of Jesus Christ.

21. As I am going out today O Lord, let my day be filled with celebration of great success in every area of my life in the name of Jesus Christ.

22. Today O Lord, I refuse to labor in vain, I will eat and enjoy the fruits of my labor in the name of Jesus Christ.

23. Whatever I do today, I will do it under open heaven in the name of Jesus Christ.
24. Today O Lord, I will be like the tree planted by rivers of water in the name of Jesus Christ.
25. Today O Lord, I will be fruitful in every area of my life in the name of Jesus Christ.
26. O God my Father, prosper the works of my hands today in the name of Jesus Christ.
27. Today my business will prosper in every area in the name of Jesus Christ.
28. O God my Father, let the former and the latter rain be released upon me today in the name of Jesus Christ.
29. O God my Father, let the former and the latter rain be released upon my business today in the name of Jesus Christ.
30. O God my Father, let the former and the latter rain be released upon my seeds today in the name of Jesus Christ.
31. O God my Father, let the former and the latter rain be released upon my field today in the name of Jesus Christ.
32. O God my Father, let the former and the latter rain be released upon the works of my hands today in the name of Jesus Christ.
33. Today I will not struggle to succeed, let the anointing of ease be released upon me now in the name of Jesus Christ.
34. Today I will not struggle to breakthrough, let the anointing of ease be released upon me now in the name of Jesus Christ.

35. Today I will not struggle to make money, let the anointing of ease be released upon now in the name of Jesus Christ.

36. Today I will not struggle before I get to the top, let the anointing of ease be released upon me now in the name of Jesus Christ.

37. O God my Father, let the people that you have prepared to contribute to my success locate me today, in the name of Jesus Christ.

38. Today I decree that this is my day, the day of testimony in the name of Jesus Christ.

39. Today I decree that this is my day, the day of miracles, signs and wonders, in the name of Jesus Christ.

40. Today I decree that this is my day, the day of fulfillment of the Word of God in my life, in the name of Jesus Christ.

41. Today I decree that this is my day, the day of the manifestation of the glory of God in every area of my life in the name of Jesus Christ.

42. Today I decree that this is my day, the day that the Lord will lift me up in the presence of everyone around me, in the name of Jesus Christ.

43. Today I decree that this is my day, the day that the Lord will permanently take away my reproach, in the name of Jesus Christ.

44. Today I decree that this is my day, the day that the Lord will permanently take away my shame in the name of Jesus Christ.

45. Today I decree that this is my day, the day that the Lord will bring to pass all His promises in my life in the name of Jesus Christ.

46. As I am going today O Lord, let the door of opportunity be opened unto me in every area in the name of Jesus Christ.
47. Today I will not miss these opportunities in the name of Jesus Christ.
48. O God my Father, order my footsteps today and guide me in every area in the name of Jesus Christ.
49. Today I will not waste my time, I will do the will of God alone in the name of Jesus Christ.
50. At the end of today, I will have reasons to be thankful and testify to the goodness of God in the name of Jesus Christ.

PRAYERS TO FIND GODLY HUSBAND

Passages To Read Before You Pray:
Genesis 2:18-25, Proverbs 18:22, Ecclesiastes 4:9-12, Psalms 30, 1, 66, 83, 128

PRAYER POINTS

1. O God my Father, I thank you for giving me the privilege to know you.
2. O God my Father, I thank you for answering my prayers whenever I cry unto you and I know that you will answer my prayer again today in the name of Jesus Christ.
3. O God my Father, I thank you for being with me all these years, for upholding me with the right hand of your righteousness.
4. I confess my sins before you today O Lord, and I plea for mercy, forgive me and cleanse me in the blood of Jesus Christ.
5. Today I will not pray in vain, my prayers will produce the desired results in the name of Jesus Christ.
6. Today I will not pray in vain, my prayers will bring uncommon testimonies in the name of Jesus Christ.
7. Today I will not pray in vain, miracles will follow my prayers in the name of Jesus Christ.
8. O God my Father, I refuse to be alone, let my helpmate locate me now in the name of Jesus Christ.

9. It is written that he that finds a wife finds a good thing; let my godly husband find me now in the name of Jesus Christ.
10. O God my Father, bless me today with a husband that will honor and cherish me in the name of Jesus Christ.
11. O God my Father, bless me today with a husband that will love me as Christ loves the church in the name of Jesus Christ.
12. O God my Father, bless me today with a husband that will love me as his own body in the name of Jesus Christ.
13. O God my Father, bless me today with a husband that his life is filled with the fear of God, in the name of Jesus Christ.
14. O God my Father, bless me today with a husband who lives a spirit filled life in the name of Jesus Christ.
15. O God my Father, bless me today with a husband that is not abusive but supportive and helpful, in the name of Jesus Christ.
16. O God my Father, bless me today with a husband that will give me freedom to serve you, so that we can both serve you in the name of Jesus Christ.
17. O God my Father, bless me today with a husband that will not kill my dream but help me to fulfill my dreams in the name of Jesus Christ.
18. O God my Father, bless me today with a man after your own heart in the name of Jesus Christ.
19. O God my Father, I refuse to make a mistake in marriage, help me to make the right decision in the name of Jesus Christ.

20. O God my Father, I refuse to make a mistake in marriage, grant me divine wisdom to make a wise decision in the name of Jesus Christ.
21. I refuse to allow the lust of the flesh to push me into making the wrong decision, in the name of Jesus Christ.
22. I refuse to allow the lust of the eyes to lure me to make the wrong decision in the name of Jesus Christ.
23. I refuse to allow anyone around me to force me into making the wrong decision in marriage, in the name of Jesus Christ.
24. I refuse to allow any situation to force me to make the wrong decision in marriage, in the name of Jesus Christ.
25. You spirit of lateness in marriage, I command you to release me now, it is my time and I am ready to get married, in the name of Jesus Christ.
26. You spirit of delay, I command you to release me now, it is my time and I am ready to get married, in the name of Jesus Christ.
27. Misfortune in every area of my life, I command you to release me now, it is my time and I am ready to get married, in the name of Jesus Christ.
28. Today I command my godly husband to come forth and locate me, in the name of Jesus Christ.
29. Today O Lord, it is high time, let my godly husband seek and find me in the name of Jesus Christ.
30. O God my Father, let my godly husband relocate to locate me in the name of Jesus Christ.
31. O God my Father, let my godly husband see your good hands upon my life in the name of Jesus Christ.
32. O God my Father, let my godly husband see your glory and honor upon my life in the name of Jesus Christ.

33. Today O Lord, put an end to loneliness in my life in the name of Jesus Christ.
34. It is written that two are better than one; bless me today with a godly husband that we can walk together in the Lord in the name of Jesus Christ.
35. It is written that two are better than one, bless me today with a godly husband that will work together to build our future, in the name of Jesus Christ.
36. O God my Father, bless me with a home that is full of love and joy, in the name of Jesus Christ.
37. O God my Father, bless me with a godly man that will not only be my husband but also my best friend forever, in the name of Jesus Christ.
38. O God my Father, bless me with a godly man that will not only be my husband but also my confidant and counselor, in the name of Jesus Christ.
39. O God my Father, bless me with a godly man that will not only be my husband but someone reliable and dependable, in the name of Jesus Christ.
40. O God my Father, bless me with a godly man that will not only be my husband but someone with vision and hardworking, in the name of Jesus Christ.
41. Every prayer that I have prayed today will produce the desired results in the name of Jesus Christ.
42. Every prayer that I have prayed today will bring forth testimonies in the name of Jesus Christ.
43. Miracles will follow my prayers in the name of Jesus Christ.
44. As I pray today, heaven will respond to my petition in the name of Jesus Christ.
45. My prayers today will bring a positive turn to my situation in the name of Jesus Christ.

PRAYERS TO FIND GOOD WIFE

Passages To Read Before You Pray:
Genesis 2:18-25, Proverbs 18:22, Ecclesiastes 4:9-12, Psalms 30, 1, 66, 83, 128

PRAYER POINTS

1. O God my Father, I thank you for giving me the privilege to know you.
2. O God my Father, I thank you for answering my prayers whenever I cry unto you and I know that you will answer my prayer again today in the name of Jesus Christ.
3. O God my Father, I thank you for being with me all these years, for upholding me with the right hand of your righteousness.
4. I confess my sins before you today O Lord, and I plea for mercy, forgive me and cleanse me in the blood of Jesus Christ.
5. Today I will not pray in vain, my prayers will produce the desired results in the name of Jesus Christ.
6. Today I will not pray in vain, my prayers will bring uncommon testimonies in the name of Jesus Christ.
7. Today I will not pray in vain, miracles will follow my prayers in the name of Jesus Christ.
8. O God my Father, I refuse to be alone, help me to locate my helpmate now in the name of Jesus Christ.

9. It is written that he finds a wife finds a good thing, help me Holy Spirit to find the good woman you have prepared for me now in the name of Jesus Christ.

10. O God my Father, bless me today with a wife that will honor and respect me in the name of Jesus Christ.

11. O God my Father, bless me today with a wife that will love me genuinely with all her heart in the name of Jesus Christ.

12. O God my Father, bless me today with a wife that will love me as her own body in the name of Jesus Christ.

13. O God my Father, bless me today with a wife whose life is filled with the fear of God, in the name of Jesus Christ.

14. O God my Father, bless me today with a wife that lives a spirit filled life in the name of Jesus Christ.

15. O God my Father, bless me today with a wife that is not abusive but supportive and helpful, in the name of Jesus Christ.

16. O God my Father, bless me today with a wife that is willing to serve you, so that we can both serve you in the name of Jesus Christ.

17. O God my Father, bless me today with a wife that will not hinder my dream but help me to fulfill my dreams in the name of Jesus Christ.

18. O God my Father, bless me today with a virtuous woman, a woman after your own heart in the name of Jesus Christ.

19. O God my Father, I refuse to make mistake in marriage, help me to make the right decision in the name of Jesus Christ.

20. O God my Father, I refuse to make mistake in marriage, grant me divine wisdom to make a wise decision in the name of Jesus Christ.

21. I refuse to allow the lust of the flesh to push me into making the wrong decision, in the name of Jesus Christ.

22. I refuse to allow the lust of the eyes to lure me to make the wrong decision in the name of Jesus Christ.

23. I refuse to allow anyone around me to force me into making the wrong decision in marriage, in the name of Jesus Christ.

24. I refuse to allow any situation to force me to make the wrong decision in marriage, in the name of Jesus Christ.

25. You spirit of lateness in marriage, I command you to release me now, it is my time and I am ready to get married, in the name of Jesus Christ.

26. You spirit of delay, I command you to release me now, it is my time and I am ready to get married, in the name of Jesus Christ.

27. Misfortune in every area of my life, I command you to release me now, it is my time and I am ready to get married, in the name of Jesus Christ.

28. Today O Lord, lead and direct me to wherever my wife is so that I may find her, in the name of Jesus Christ.

29. Today O Lord, it is high time, let my good wife seek and find me in the name of Jesus Christ.

30. O God my Father, let my good wife relocate to locate me in the name of Jesus Christ.

31. O God my Father, let my good wife see your good hands upon my life in the name of Jesus Christ.

32. O God my Father, let my good wife see your glory and honor upon my life in the name of Jesus Christ.

33. Today O Lord, put an end to loneliness in my life in the name of Jesus Christ.

34. It is written that two are better than one, bless me today with a good wife that we can walk together in the Lord in the name of Jesus Christ.

35. It is written that two are better than one, bless me today with a good wife that will work together to build our future, in the name of Jesus Christ.

36. O God my Father, bless me with a home that is full of love and joy, in the name of Jesus Christ.

37. O God my Father, bless me with a good wife that will not only be my wife but also my best friend forever, in the name of Jesus Christ.

38. O God my Father, bless me with a good wife that will not only be my wife but also my confidant and counselor, in the name of Jesus Christ.

39. O God my Father, bless me with a good wife that will not only be my wife but someone reliable and dependable, in the name of Jesus Christ.

40. O God my Father, bless me with a good wife that will not only be my wife but a virtuous woman and hardworking, in the name of Jesus Christ.

41. Every prayer that I have prayed today will produce the desired results in the name of Jesus Christ.

42. Every prayer that I have prayed today will bring forth testimonies in the name of Jesus Christ.

43. Miracles will follow my prayers in the name of Jesus Christ.

44. As I pray today, heaven will respond to my petition in the name of Jesus Christ.

45. My prayers today will bring a positive turn around into my situation in the name of Jesus Christ.

DELIVERANCE FROM CANCER

Passages To Read Before You Pray:
John 14:14, Psalms 6, 9, 30, 88, Isaiah 53

PRAYER POINTS:

1. I cover myself in the precious blood of Jesus Christ.
2. O God my Father, let the blood of Jesus flow from the crown of my head to the soles of my feet in the name of Jesus Christ.
3. O God my Father, forgive me of anything that I have done in the past that brought this plague on me, in the name of Jesus Christ.
4. With all my heart, I forgive anyone that has hurt me, in the name of Jesus Christ.
5. O God my Father, send your Word and heal me from cancer in the name of Jesus Christ.
6. O God my Father, send your Word and deliver me from the sting of cancer in the name of Jesus Christ.
7. Every unusual and unregulated growth in my body, I command you to be destroyed in the name of Jesus Christ.
8. O God my Father, empower my immune system to fight and kill every unusual growth in my body system, in the name of Jesus Christ.
9. O God my Father, empower my immune system to fight and kill every evil growth in my body system, in the name of Jesus Christ.
10. O God my Father, empower my immune system to fight and destroy every cell in my body that is cancerous, in the name of Jesus Christ.

11. Cancer is not for me, it is of the devil, I hereby reject cancer and I command you to die now in the name of Jesus Christ.
12. Cancer, you have no right to torment me, my body is the temple of the Holy Spirit, get out and be destroyed in the name of Jesus Christ.
13. Any uncontrollable growth in any part of my body, receive the fire of God and die permanently in the name of Jesus Christ.
14. Every evil invader in any part of my body system, receive the fire of God and die permanently in the name of Jesus Christ.
15. Every seed of cancer in any part of my body, I command you to dry out and be destroyed in the name of Jesus Christ.
16. Spirit of cancer, you cannot kill me because my life is in the hands of God in the name of Jesus Christ.
17. It does not matter what has happened in the past, cancer will not succeed over my life, I belong to God, in the name of Jesus Christ.
18. Spirit of cancer, I command you to loose your hold over my life in the name of Jesus Christ.
19. I command every evil spread of cancer in my body to receive the fire of God and die now, in the name of Jesus Christ.
20. Spirit of cancer, you are no longer permitted to torment me, get out of my life and be destroyed in the name of Jesus Christ.
21. Spirit of cancer, you are not allowed to take my life, you cannot take what you cannot give, in the name of Jesus Christ.

22. Hereditary problems that lead to the development of cancer, loose your hold upon me in the name of Jesus Christ, my life is precious to God.

23. Self-inflicted problems that lead to the development of cancer, loose your hold upon me, be destroyed by the fire of God in the name of Jesus Christ.

24. Environmental problems that lead to the development of cancer, loose your hold upon me in the name of Jesus Christ, my life is too precious to God.

25. Any trace or sign of cancer in my body system, I command you to disappear in the name of Jesus Christ.

26. Every evil discovery in my body be destroyed, by the fire of God in the name of Jesus Christ.

27. O God my Father, let the divine treatment begin now in every part of my body in the name of Jesus Christ.

28. O God my Father, let the process of divine chemotherapy begin now in every part of my body, in the name of Jesus Christ.

29. O God my Father, let there be divine surgery in any part of my body where it is needed in the name of Jesus Christ.

30. O God my Father, let there be an instant healing in the affected part of my body in the name of Jesus Christ.

31. I reject every evil doctor's report, I only believe the report of the Lord in the name of Jesus Christ.

32. O God my Father, dispatch heavenly doctors to work with my doctors for my complete and permanent healing in the name of Jesus Christ.

33. O God my Father, by your grace and mercy, I am 100% cancer free in the name of Jesus Christ.

34. As from today, every doctor's report will bring me joy in the name of Jesus Christ.

35. I reject bad news from my doctors, I shall receive good news in the name of Jesus Christ.
36. O God my Father, let my health bring glory and honor to your name in the name of Jesus Christ.
37. Any form of cancer will have no place in my body in the name of Jesus Christ.
38. Every dead organ in my body, I command you to receive the life of God and live in the name of Jesus Christ.
39. Every organ in my body that malfunctions, I command you to function properly in the name of Jesus Christ.
40. I command every part of my body to reject sicknesses and diseases, in the name of Jesus Christ.
41. Today I claim long life and good health in the name of Jesus Christ.
42. Today I receive wisdom to eat well with good diets in the name of Jesus Christ.
43. Spirit of cancer, I am no longer your candidate in the name of Jesus Christ.
44. Spirit of infirmity, I am no longer your candidate in the name of Jesus Christ.
45. Today, I am totally delivered from cancer in the name of Jesus Christ.
46. The power of God sets me free and I am free indeed, in the name of Jesus Christ.
47. My body is the temple of the Holy Spirit, it cannot be defiled by cancer in the name of Jesus Christ.
48. O God my Father, let my testimony of victory over cancer begin now in the name of Jesus Christ.
49. I am covered in the blood of Jesus Christ, cancer will never come back, I am free in the name of Jesus Christ.
50. O God my Father, I thank you for perfect and complete healing from cancer in the name of Jesus Christ.

MY HARVEST SHALL CONTINUE

Passages To Read Before You Pray:
Judges 6:1-40, Deuteronomy 28:1-13, 30:9, Leviticus 26:5,
Isaiah 30:23, Amos 9:13

PRAYER POINTS

1. O God my Father, I thank you for being my God.
2. O God my Father, I thank you for your provision and protection over me and my household.
3. O God my Father, forgive me of all my sins and errors, and cleanse me in the blood of Jesus Christ.
4. Holy Spirit of God, intervene in the affairs of my life and let there be a positive turn around, in the name of Jesus Christ.
5. Anything that I will do, that will allow enemies to frustrate my life, Father Lord, deliver me from it in the name of Jesus Christ.
6. I am covered in the blood of Jesus Christ, my enemies will not prevail against me in the name of Jesus Christ.
7. We are covered in the blood of Jesus Christ, the enemies will not prevail against my family, in the name of Jesus Christ.
8. I am covered in the blood of Jesus Christ, my enemies will not prevail against my harvest, in the name of Jesus Christ.
9. I am covered in the blood of Jesus Christ, my enemies will not prevail against my finances in the name of Jesus Christ.

10. I am covered in the blood of Jesus Christ, my enemies will not prevail against the sources of my income in the name of Jesus Christ.
11. I am covered in the blood of Jesus Christ, my enemies will not prevail against my destiny in the name of Jesus Christ.
12. I am covered in the blood of Jesus Christ, my enemies will not prevail against my dreams in the name of Jesus Christ.
13. I am covered in the blood of Jesus Christ, my enemies will not prevail against my marriage in the name of Jesus Christ.
14. O God my Father, deliver me from the hands of the wicked attacking my harvest, in the name of Jesus Christ.
15. O God my Father, deliver me from the hands of the wicked destroying my harvest in the name of Jesus Christ.
16. O God my Father, deliver me from the hands of the wicked robbing me of my harvest in the name of Jesus Christ.
17. I come against all invaders attacking my harvest, you will not escape the judgment of God, in the name of Jesus Christ.
18. I come against all invaders attacking my business, you will not escape the judgment of God, in the name of Jesus Christ.
19. I come against all invaders attacking my finances, you will not escape the judgment of God in the name of Jesus Christ.

20. I come against all invaders attacking my employment, you will not escape the judgment of God in the name of Jesus Christ.
21. I come against all invaders attacking the sources of my income, you will not escape the judgment of God in the name of Jesus Christ.
22. I come against all invaders attacking my family, you will not escape the judgment of God in the name of Jesus Christ.
23. I come against all invaders attacking my joy, you will not escape the judgment of God in the name of Jesus Christ.
24. I come against all invaders attacking my spouse, you will not escape the judgment of God in the name of Jesus Christ.
25. I come against all invaders attacking my children, you will not escape the judgment of God in the name of Jesus Christ.
26. I come against all invaders attacking my marriage, you will not escape the judgment of God in the name of Jesus Christ.
27. Any power anywhere hired to destroy my harvest, you will not prosper in the name of Jesus Christ.
28. Any power anywhere hired to scatter my harvest, you will not prosper in the name of Jesus Christ.
29. Any power anywhere hired to waste my harvest, you will not prosper in the name of Jesus Christ.
30. Any power anywhere hired to destroy the works of my hands, you will not prosper in the name of Jesus Christ.
31. I refuse to labor in vain in the name of Jesus Christ.
32. I will eat the fruits of my labor in the name of Jesus Christ.

33. I will not work for another to eat in the name of Jesus Christ.
34. I speak increase into my harvest in the name of Jesus Christ.
35. My harvest shall be plenteous according to the Word of God in the name of Jesus Christ.
36. My field shall bring forth fruits in abundance in the name of Jesus Christ.
37. No matter the situation around me, my harvest will continue in the name of Jesus Christ.
38. No matter the situation of the economy, my harvest will not be negatively affected in the name of Jesus Christ.
39. O God my Father, deliver me today from the hands of the oppressors in the name of Jesus Christ.
40. O God my Father, oppress my oppressors in the name of Jesus Christ.
41. O God my Father, visit my land and make my land beautiful in the name of Jesus Christ.
42. No matter the situation of the economy, my finances will not be negatively affected in the name of Jesus Christ.
43. No matter the situation of the economy, my income will not be negatively affected in the name of Jesus Christ.
44. No matter the situation of the economy, my family will not be negatively affected in the name of Jesus Christ.
45. No matter the situation of the economy, my business will not be negatively affected in the name of Jesus Christ.
46. O God my Father, release upon me now the former rain and the latter rain and let my harvest begin, in the name of Jesus Christ.
47. My seeds will not die, my seeds shall bring desired harvest in the name of Jesus Christ.

48. O God my Father, let there be divine protection upon my harvest against the harvest destroyers in the name of Jesus Christ.
49. Harvest destroyers, I am a child of the Kingdom, you have no right to destroy my harvest in the name of Jesus Christ.
50. My harvest shall multiply in thousand folds in the name of Jesus Christ.

FATHER, MAKE ME YOUR FAVORITE CHILD

Passages To Read Before You Pray:
Isaiah 43:4-7, Psalm 2, 30, 42, Acts 13:22

PRAYER POINTS

1. O God my Father, I thank you for giving me this great privilege to be called your child.
2. O God my Father, I thank you for always being there for me and my family.
3. I cover myself and my household in the precious blood of Jesus Christ.
4. O God my Father, grant me unusual favor in every area of my life in the name of Jesus Christ.
5. O God my Father, make me a favorite child, like King David, in the name of Jesus Christ.
6. O God my Father, give me the grace to obey you at all times in the name of Jesus Christ.
7. O God my Father, give me the grace to do your will alone, in the name of Jesus Christ.
8. O God my Father, make me a man/woman after your own heart like David, in the name of Jesus Christ.
9. O God my Father, make me a favorite child of the Father like Joseph, in the name of Jesus Christ.
10. O God my Father, be with me in every situation of life as you were with Joseph, in the name of Jesus Christ.
11. O God my Father, show me your mercy and give me favor in the sight of everyone around me, in the name of Jesus Christ.

12. In any situation I find myself, I will stand out; I refuse to blend in with the crowd in the name of Jesus Christ.
13. O God my Father, prosper the works of my hands as you did unto Joseph, in the name of Jesus Christ.
14. O God my Father, make me a favorite child of the king like Daniel, in the name of Jesus Christ.
15. O God my Father, grant me favor even in the sight of my enemies, in the name of Jesus Christ.
16. O God my Father, promote and take me to the top in this land as you did unto Daniel in the land of Babylon, in the name of Jesus Christ.
17. O God my Father, manifest your power in my life as you did with Daniel in the land of Babylon that people around may know that I serve the Living God, in the name of Jesus Christ.
18. O God my Father, give me victory over all my enemies as you did unto Daniel in the land of Babylon, in the name of Jesus Christ.
19. O God my Father, give me an excellent Spirit that will take me to the top as you did unto Daniel in the land of Babylon, in the name of Jesus Christ.
20. O God my Father, make me a source of blessing to this generation as you did unto Daniel in the land of Babylon, in the name of Jesus Christ.

DELIVERANCE FROM IMPOSSIBILITY

Passages To Read Before You Pray:
Luke 1:37, Job 42:2, Psalm 115, 135, Isaiah 43:13, Habakkuk 3:6, Matthew 19:26

PRAYER POINTS

1. O God my Father, I thank you for being a wonderful and marvelous God and an awesome friend.
2. Father Lord, I thank you for always being there for me and for demonstrating your power in every area of my life.
3. O God my Father, forgive me today of all my sins and errors, cleanse me from all unrighteousness in the name of Jesus Christ.
4. I cover myself and my household in the blood of Jesus Christ.
5. O God my Father, release into my life today divine resources and let my life bring forth uncommon harvest, in the name of Jesus Christ.
6. I receive the grace of God to fulfill the divine plan for my life; I will not fall into the plan of the enemy in the name of Jesus Christ.
7. I hereby destroy every plan of the enemy concerning my life in the name of Jesus Christ.
8. O God my Father, give me divine support to fulfill all my plans and dreams, in the name of Jesus Christ.
9. O God my Father, give me divine guidance in every area so that I will not miss my way, in the name of Jesus Christ.

10. O God my Father, reveal yourself unto me today through your name that is called Jehovah, in the name of Jesus Christ.
11. O God my Father, reveal yourself unto me today as Jehovah Jireh; the Great Provider, in the name of Jesus Christ.
12. O God my Father, reveal yourself unto me today as Jehovah Nissi; the Man of War, in the name of Jesus Christ.
13. O God my Father, let me experience you by your name, in the name of Jesus Christ.
14. I hereby stand and declare, Satan cannot and will not rob me of my kingdom benefits, in the name of Jesus Christ.
15. Because I know my God, I will be strong and do great exploits in the name of Jesus Christ.
16. O God my Father, do something extraordinarily good in my life today in the name of Jesus Christ.
17. O God my Father, do something supernatural in my life today in the name of Jesus Christ.
18. I receive the grace of God to operate at the realm of the supernatural, in the name of Jesus Christ.
19. I receive the grace of God to overcome all impossibilities in my life, in the name of Jesus Christ.
20. O God my Father, let your supernatural power reverse the irreversible in every area of my life, in the name of Jesus Christ.
21. O God my Father, let your supernatural power move the immovable in every area of my life, in the name of Jesus Christ.
22. By your mighty hands O Lord, let every irreversible be reversed, and immovable be moved in every area of my life, in the name of Jesus Christ.

23. O God my Father, let every physical and spiritual challenge in my life be resolved today, in the name of Jesus Christ.
24. Today O Lord, let everything that seems impossible be possible unto me in the name of Jesus Christ.
25. By the authority in the name of Jesus Christ, what I found most impossible to accomplish will become possible for me.
26. Every chain of impossibility around my situation is broken today, in the name of Jesus Christ.
27. From this moment onward, I will experience possibilities in every area of my life in the name of Jesus Christ.
28. O God my Father, let there be light in every area of my life and let darkness flee, in the name of Jesus Christ.
29. O God my Father, set me apart by your grace and by the Holy Ghost, to fulfill my assignment and calling in the name of Jesus Christ.
30. O God my Father, give me the grace to understand what you are saying at this moment and about this moment, in the name of Jesus Christ.
31. O God my Father, I am listening, speak to me about my situation that I may know what to do, in the name of Jesus Christ.
32. O God my Father, give me the grace to hear what the Spirit is saying and to follow your instructions, that I may be victorious in every area of life in the name of Jesus Christ.
33. O God my Father, speak to me, I want to know about my next step in life, in the name of Jesus Christ.
34. O God my Father, let my prayers provoke heaven to speak and fight on my behalf, in the name of Jesus Christ.

35. O God my Father, by faith I receive a Word for this moment in my life, a Word of hope and comfort in the name of Jesus Christ.

36. O God my Father, give me the grace to make right and wise choices in life, in the name of Jesus Christ.

37. O God my Father, correct me when necessary so that I will not make wrong decisions in life, in the name of Jesus Christ.

38. I will not be a misfit for the heavenly kingdom in the name of Jesus Christ.

39. Today O Lord, I voluntarily submit my will, I ask you to take charge of my life in the name of Jesus Christ.

40. O God my Father, I give up my will and I ask you to take absolute control of my life and situation, in the name of Jesus Christ.

41. From this moment O Lord, I ask you to help me make all my decisions in the name of Jesus Christ.

42. Today O God my Father, I put the government of my life upon your shoulder in the name of Jesus Christ.

43. O God my Father, let your fire consume everything you do not approve in my life, in the name of Jesus Christ.

44. O God my Father, deposit your fire upon my life to fulfill my divine assignment in the name of Jesus Christ.

45. O God my Father, deposit your fire upon me to purify my life in every area, in the name of Jesus Christ.

46. O God my Father, deposit your fire upon me and let my yoke be destroyed in the name of Jesus Christ.

47. O God my Father, I am ready to go on the mission that you sent me, deposit your fire upon me to prepare and equip me for the ministry in the name of Jesus Christ.

48. O God my Father, deposit your fire upon me, empower me to liberate the captives in the name of Jesus Christ.

49. O God my Father, let your fire come upon me, let every satanic chain and rope holding me be destroyed, in the name of Jesus Christ.
50. O God my Father, deposit your fire upon me, fire to cast out devils in the name of Jesus Christ.
51. O God my Father, deposit your fire upon me, fire to heal the sick in the name of Jesus Christ.
52. O God my Father, deposit your fire upon me, fire of revival in the name of Jesus Christ.
53. O God my Father, deposit your fire upon me, fire to work miracles in the name of Jesus Christ.
54. O God my Father, release your fire upon me today and make me a flaming fire in the name of Jesus Christ.
55. O God my Father, release your fire upon me today and make me untouchable to my enemies, in the name of Jesus Christ.
56. The fire of God in me will not die, in the name of Jesus Christ.
57. O God my Father, let every evil counsel against me be frustrated and cancelled in the name of Jesus Christ.
58. O God my Father, let my enemies bend their rules in my favor, in the name of Jesus Christ.
59. O God my Father, let people that will decide on my advancement bend their rules in my favor, in the name of Jesus Christ.
60. O God my Father, let the agreement of the enemies over my life be frustrated and disappointed, in the name of Jesus Christ.
61. O God my Father, let your counsel prevail over my life, not the desires of my enemies, in the name of Jesus Christ.

62. O God my Father, let me find favor before kings and princes like Moses, in the name of Jesus Christ.
63. From this moment onward, O God my Father, let my enemies work in my favor in the name of Jesus Christ.
64. O God my Father, convince my greatest enemy to become my strongest supporter in the name of Jesus Christ.
65. O God my Father, convince my enemies to channel all their resources to support me, in the name of Jesus Christ.
66. From today onward O God my Father, let my enemies begin to fight for me, even with their lives in the name of Jesus Christ.
67. O God my Father, have your way in the affairs of my life, in the name of Jesus Christ.
68. Today, my heavens are open in the name of Jesus Christ.
69. O God my Father, let the former and the latter rain begin to fall into every area of my life, in the name of Jesus Christ.
70. I hereby speak into existence all the blessings that God has prepared for me in heavenly places, in the name of Jesus Christ.

FATHER, MANIFEST YOURSELF IN ME

Passages To Read Before You Pray:
Ephesians 3:20-21, Psalms 19, 29, 30, Isaiah 42:8, 60:1-22

PRAYER POINTS

1. O God my Father, I thank you for always being there for me and with me.
2. O God my Father, forgive me of all my sins, iniquities and wrong doings, cleanse me in the precious blood of Jesus Christ, in the name of Jesus Christ.
3. I cover myself and my household in the precious blood of Jesus Christ.
4. O God my Father, demonstrate your power in my life as you did in the days of Elijah the prophet, in the name of Jesus Christ.
5. O God my Father, let my life be a living proof for the whole world that you are a great deliverer, in the name of Jesus Christ.
6. O God my Father, manifest yourself in my life as the Lion of the tribe of Judah, and render every satanic lion powerless and useless in the name of Jesus Christ.
7. O God my Father, use me as you did unto Elijah the prophet to demonstrate to the world that you are the consuming fire who answers by fire, in the name of Jesus Christ.
8. O God my Father, in my very limited state, demonstrate your infiniteness in the name of Jesus Christ.
9. I receive the grace of God today to overtake those who have gone ahead of me, in the name of Jesus Christ.

10. Laziness, fear and doubt causing me to limit what God can do, get out of my life now in the name of Jesus Christ.

11. I receive the grace of God and the anointing to positively affect my generation, in the name of Jesus Christ.

12. O God my Father, use me to make a statement to the world in greatness, achievement, prosperity and anointing in the name of Jesus Christ.

13. O God my Father, release your fire upon me and let my Goliath drop dead, in the name of Jesus Christ.

14. O God my Father, as I lift up my hands and voice to you in prayer, let the east wind blow and make a way in my Red Sea, in the name of Jesus Christ.

15. O God my Father, as I shout hallelujah to your name, let the foundation of my walls of Jericho crumble and fall down flat, in the name of Jesus Christ.

16. O God my Father, as I enter into the Lion's den, let the hungry lions become vegetable for my sake, in the name of Jesus Christ.

GOD'S BATTLE AXE

Passages To Read Before You Pray:
Jeremiah 51:20-64, 1:8-10, Proverbs 18:21, Philippians 2:9-11,
Revelation 12:11

PRAYER POINTS

1. O God my Father, I thank you for being a wonderful God, a good Father, and an awesome friend.
2. O God my Father, thank you for always being there for me and my household.
3. O God my Father, forgive me of my sins and iniquities, overlook my errors and mistakes in the name of Jesus Christ.
4. I cover myself and my household in the precious blood of Jesus Christ.
5. As a battle axe for the Lord, I destroy every evil network working on my case, in the name of Jesus Christ.
6. As God's weapon of war, I scatter all evil collaboration that is against me in the name of Jesus Christ.
7. As God's weapon of war, I destroy every satanic manifestation and establishment against my life in the name of Jesus Christ.
8. Today I pronounce death penalty upon all household wickedness fighting against my destiny, in the name of Jesus Christ.
9. By the authority in the name of Jesus Christ, I pull down and destroy every demonic throne erected against me in the name of Jesus Christ.

10. With the blood of Jesus Christ, I neutralize every poison passed into my system through the food I have eaten in the dream, in the name of Jesus Christ.
11. Today I pull down and destroy all evil altar erected against me in the name of Jesus Christ.
12. I hereby pronounce death penalty upon every power trying to contaminate my blessings, in the name of Jesus Christ.
13. Every evil voice working against me, the Lord rebuke you and put you to silence today, in the name of Jesus Christ.
14. I condemn every evil mouth and tongue rising against me in the name of Jesus Christ.
15. As a battle axe for the Lord, I destroy every power standing in my way, hindering me from moving forward, in the name of Jesus Christ.
16. By the power in the blood of Jesus Christ, I destroy every soul-tie giving the enemies, legal ground in my life in the name of Jesus Christ.
17. Today I withdraw access and pass that I have innocently or ignorantly given to the enemy, in the name of Jesus Christ.
18. I hereby terminate every agreement that I have innocently or ignorantly signed with the enemy, in the name of Jesus Christ.
19. I hereby terminate the right of ownership claimed by the enemies, over my life in the name of Jesus Christ.
20. I hereby terminate the right of ownership claimed by the enemies, over the life of my spouse in the name of Jesus Christ.

21. I hereby terminate the right of ownership claimed by the enemies, over the life of my children in the name of Jesus Christ.
22. I hereby terminate the right of ownership claimed by the enemies, over my finances in the name of Jesus Christ.
23. I hereby terminate the right of ownership claimed by the enemies, over my marriage in the name of Jesus Christ.
24. I hereby terminate the right of ownership claimed by the enemies, over my ministry in the name of Jesus Christ.
25. I hereby terminate the right of ownership claimed by the enemies, over my business in the name of Jesus Christ.
26. I hereby terminate the right of ownership claimed by the enemies, over my destiny in the name of Jesus Christ.
27. I hereby terminate the right of ownership claimed by the enemies, over my dreams and future in the name of Jesus Christ.
28. I hereby terminate the right of ownership claimed by the enemies, over my breakthroughs in the name of Jesus Christ.
29. I hereby terminate the right of ownership claimed by the enemies, over my properties in the name of Jesus Christ.
30. Today I cancel every mission accomplished by the enemies over my life, in the name of Jesus Christ.

I WILL NOT SINK

Passages To Read Before You Pray:
2 Kings 6:1-7, Isaiah 43:1-4, Psalms 46, 59, 69, 70, Matthew
14:22-33

PRAYER POINTS

1. O God my Father, I thank you for always being there for me.
2. Father Lord, I thank you for holding me with your right hand of righteous, telling me that I should not be afraid.
3. I hereby confess my sins today, I pray that you forgive me and cleanse me in the precious blood of Jesus Christ.
4. I cover myself and my family in the blood of Jesus Christ.
5. O God my Father, let your mercy prevail against the judgment in every area of my life, in the name of Jesus Christ.
6. O God my Father, let the supernatural combined with my natural efforts bring superior results, in the name of Jesus Christ.
7. O God my Father, let my limited abilities combined with the unlimited abilities of God bring outstanding results in my life, in the name of Jesus Christ.
8. O God my Father, dip your mighty hands into the evil rivers swallowing my glory and let my glory come to physical manifestation, in the name of Jesus Christ.
9. O God my Father, let your supernatural power come into my situation and let there be a positive turn around, in the name of Jesus Christ.

10. O God my Father, demonstrate your power in my life and let my missing blessings be found, in the name of Jesus Christ.
11. O God my Father, dip your mighty hands into my life and let my hidden potentials come to light, in the name of Jesus Christ.
12. O God my Father, dip your mighty hands into my life and let my hidden possibilities begin to manifest, in the name of Jesus Christ.
13. O God my Father, dip your mighty hands into my life and let my hidden miracles come to light, in the name of Jesus Christ.
14. I command my hidden talents to come to physical manifestation now, in the name of Jesus Christ.
15. I command my hidden abilities to come to physical manifestation now, in the name of Jesus Christ.
16. I command my hidden glory to come to physical manifestation now, in the name of Jesus Christ.
17. I command my hidden breakthroughs to come to physical manifestation now, in the name of Jesus Christ.
18. I command every imprisoned promotion in my life to come to physical manifestation now, in the name of Jesus Christ.
19. I command my buried prosperity to come to physical manifestation now, in the name of Jesus Christ.
20. O God my Father, give me the grace to truly discover myself, in the name of Jesus Christ.
21. O God my Father, give me the grace to truly discover my worth, value, and potential in your kingdom in the name of Jesus Christ.
22. O God my Father, give me the grace to truly discover your purpose for my life, in the name of Jesus Christ.

23. I have Jesus Christ in my boat, I will not be drowned even in the stormy weather, in the name of Jesus Christ.
24. No matter the situation around me, I will stay afloat like the axe head in the name of Jesus Christ.
25. When people are sinking all around me because of the challenges of life, I will not sink, I will stay afloat in the name of Jesus Christ.
26. No matter the storm and turbulence around me, I will not be afraid, in Christ Jesus I find my resting place, in the name of Jesus Christ.
27. Jesus Christ is my foundation, I cannot be moved in the name of Jesus Christ.
28. I receive the grace of God to overcome every situation and problem in my life, and to testify to the goodness of the Lord in the name of Jesus Christ.
29. My problems cannot swallow me, Jesus is my Lord.
30. I will not sink because my God is holding me with His right hand of righteousness, in the name of Jesus Christ.
31. Because Jesus Christ walked on water, I cannot sink.
32. Irrespective of negative circumstances around me, I will stay afloat in the name of Jesus Christ.
33. I am coming out victorious no matter what, in the name of Jesus Christ.

MY VOICE SHALL BE HEARD

Passages To Read Before You Pray:
Proverbs 1:24-33, Psalms 29, 50, 102

PRAYER POINTS

1. O God my Father, I thank you for being a faithful God in my life.
2. O God my Father, forgive me of all my sins and wrong doings, let the blood of Jesus Christ cleanse me and make me whole, in the name of Jesus Christ.
3. I hereby cover myself and my household in the precious blood of Jesus Christ.
4. O God my Father, let the people that you have prepared to help me hear my voice today and attend to my situation, in the name of Jesus Christ.
5. O God my Father, let the people that you have prepared to contribute to my success hear my voice today and help me to achieve my goal, in the name of Jesus Christ.
6. O God my Father, let the people that you have prepared to rescue me out of this pit of hopelessness hear my voice today and come for my rescue in the name of Jesus Christ.
7. O God my Father, let the people that you have prepared to lead me to the top hear my voice today and show me the way, in the name of Jesus Christ.
8. O God my Father, let the people that you have prepared to introduce me to the right people hear my voice today and show me love, in the name of Jesus Christ.

9. O God my Father, let the time of my favor come, in the name of Jesus Christ.
10. O God my Father, order my steps to cross paths with my helpers, in the name of Jesus Christ.
11. O God my Father, let my helpers listen to me and attend to my needs, in the name of Jesus Christ.
12. O God my Father, let my voice be the voice everyone must hear and attend to, in the name of Jesus Christ.
13. O God my Father, let my voice that has been shunned for years get the attention of my helpers, in the name of Jesus Christ.
14. From this moment onward, my voice will be heard and I will never be the same again, in the name of Jesus Christ.
15. O God my Father, send a messenger of joy to reverse any evil agenda put in place for me, in the name of Jesus Christ.
16. O God my Father, give me the grace to listen and obey your voice, in the name of Jesus Christ.
17. Anything in my life hindering my voice from being heard, Father Lord, remove it now, in the name of Jesus Christ.
18. Anything that I have done hindering my voice from being heard, Father Lord, forgive me today, in the name of Jesus Christ.
19. O God my Father, give me the grace to do your will, that I will not miss the day of my favor, in the name of Jesus Christ.
20. O God my Father, prevent me from doing anything that will cause my voice not to be heard, in the name of Jesus Christ.

DELIVERANCE FROM EVIL NAME ASSOCIATION

Passages To Read Before You Pray:
1 Chronicles 4:9-10, Genesis 25:24-26, 1 Samuel 25:1-25

PRAYER POINTS

1. O God my Father, I thank you for your Word that is yes and amen, and is forever settled in heaven.
2. O God my Father, I thank you for standing by your Words that you have spoken into my life and you will bring it to pass in the name of Jesus Christ.
3. I confess my sins today O Lord, I pray that you forgive me and cleanse me in the blood of Jesus Christ.
4. I cover myself and my household in the precious blood of Jesus Christ.
5. I cover the works of my hands in the blood of Jesus Christ.
6. Today I declare, no evil shall come near my family, nor any danger come near my household, we are well protected by the Lord and covered under His wings in the name of Jesus Christ.
7. I will not be brought down by the enemy's fire, in the name of Jesus Christ.
8. My success will not work against me in the name of Jesus Christ.
9. My success will not push me to rebel against God, in the name of Jesus Christ.
10. I will not be manipulated to relax when I am supposed to work or fight, in the name of Jesus Christ.
11. I hereby cover my name in the blood of Jesus Christ.

12. By the authority in the name of Jesus Christ, I destroy any link between my name and any evil spirit or idol, in the name of Jesus Christ.

13. By the authority in the name of Jesus Christ, I destroy any link between my children's name and any evil spirit or idol, in the name of Jesus Christ.

14. By the authority in the name of Jesus Christ, I destroy any link between my spouse's name and any evil spirit or idol, in the name of Jesus Christ.

15. I refuse to advertise or glorify any evil spirit or idol through my name, in the name of Jesus Christ.

16. Every legal ground of the enemy in my life because of my name, I claim it back by the fire of God in the name of Jesus Christ.

17. Every power affecting my life because of my name, loose your hold over my life now, in the name of Jesus Christ.

18. Every power affecting my activities because of my name, loose your hold upon my life now, in the name of Jesus Christ.

19. Every power affecting my success because of my name, loose your hold upon my life, in the name of Jesus Christ.

20. Every power affecting my progress because of my name, loose your hold upon my life, in the name of Jesus Christ.

21. Every power delaying my breakthroughs because of my name, loose your hold upon my life now, in the name of Jesus Christ.

22. Every power hindering my miracles because of my name, loose your hold upon my life now, in the name of Jesus Christ.

23. My name will not hinder the fulfillment of my destiny, in the name of Jesus Christ.
24. My name will not hinder my miracles, in the name of Jesus Christ.
25. My name will not hinder my testimony, in the name of Jesus Christ.
26. My name will not hinder my success in the name of Jesus Christ.
27. My name will not attract evil into my life, in the name of Jesus Christ.
28. My name will not attract failure into my life, in the name of Jesus Christ.
29. My name will not attract poverty into my life, in the name of Jesus Christ.
30. My name shall attract favor from every area, in the name of Jesus Christ.
31. My name shall attract open heavens, in the name of Jesus Christ.
32. Everyone that hears my name shall arise to help me, in the name of Jesus Christ.
33. I destroy any association between my name and any idol, in the name of Jesus Christ.
34. I destroy any association between my name and any evil spirit, in the name of Jesus Christ.
35. I destroy any association between my name and any strange god, in the name of Jesus Christ.
36. I destroy any association between my name and poverty, in the name of Jesus Christ.
37. I destroy any association between my name and the spirit of the dead, in the name of Jesus Christ.
38. I destroy any association between my name and the spirit of death, in the name of Jesus Christ.

39. I reject every evil attached to my first name, you will not have any effect over my life in the name of Jesus Christ.
40. I reject every evil attached to my last name, you will not have any effect over my life in the name of Jesus Christ.
41. I reject every evil attached to my middle name, you will not have any effect over my life in the name of Jesus Christ.
42. I reject every evil attached to my family name, you will not have any effect over my life in the name of Jesus Christ.
43. Today I link my name with my Father and my God Jehovah, in the name of Jesus Christ.
44. I refuse to bear any name promoting other gods, in the name of Jesus Christ.
45. Whenever and wherever my name is mentioned, the name of the Lord will be promoted, in the name of Jesus Christ.
46. O God my Father, bring out Israel that is in me, in the name of Jesus Christ.
47. I command my glory and authority as a prince to manifest now in the name of Jesus Christ.
48. O God my Father, let my neglected and ignored life become the most sought after, in the name of Jesus Christ.
49. I refuse to disappoint myself and my unborn generation, in the name of Jesus Christ.
50. I rebel against and reject whatever evil that this society and generation have prepared for me, in the name of Jesus Christ.
51. I refuse to struggle to make progress in life, in the name of Jesus Christ.

52. O God my Father, let the Israel in me manifest by your fire, I want to fulfill purpose in life, in the name of Jesus Christ.
53. I will not die with my Israel buried inside of me, in the name of Jesus Christ.
54. I will be what God has planned me to be, in the name of Jesus Christ.
55. O God my Father, let my name change from Jacob to Israel today, in the name of Jesus Christ.

BEFORE YOU ENTER INTO THE NEW YEAR

Passages To Read Before You Pray:
Habakkuk 1:5, Joel 2:21-26, Job 5:8-11, Psalm 126

PRAYER POINTS

1. Father Lord, I thank you for bringing me this far and knowing you will not depart from me, in the name of Jesus Christ.
2. Father Lord, I thank you for the privilege to see this moment, the end of this year, in the name of Jesus Christ.
3. I confess all the sins that I have committed and mistakes that I have made in this outgoing year, Lord have mercy, forgive me and cleanse me in the blood of Jesus Christ.
4. I receive the grace of God and the anointing of the Holy Spirit to succeed in every area in this New Year, in the name of Jesus Christ.
5. Problems that always roll over with me from year to year, I command you to stop right here right now, you will not go with me into the New Year, in the name of Jesus Christ.
6. Every power that is trying to make my God a liar in the New Year, depart from me now and never come back in the name of Jesus Christ.
7. Every power that always robs me of the New Year's blessings, you are no longer allowed to do so, loose your hold upon my life now in the name of Jesus Christ.

8. O God my Father, let the Red Sea of this outgoing year take away my Pharaoh and his army forever, I shall see them no more in the name of Jesus Christ.

9. Spirit of failure, you have tormented me long enough, this is the end of your game, I shall see you no more in the name of Jesus Christ.

10. Spirit of poverty, you have tormented me long enough, this is the end of your game, I shall see you no more in the name of Jesus Christ.

11. Spirit of stagnancy, you have tormented me long enough, this is the end of your game, I shall see you no more in the name of Jesus Christ.

12. Spirit of misfortune, you have tormented me long enough, this is the end of your game, I shall see you no more in the name of Jesus Christ.

13. Household wickedness, you have tormented me long enough, this is the end of your game, I shall see you no more in the name of Jesus Christ.

14. Destiny killers, you have tormented me long enough, this is the end of your game, I shall see you no more in the name of Jesus Christ.

15. Spirit of rejection, you have tormented me long enough, this is the end of your game, I shall see you no more in the name of Jesus Christ.

16. Spirit of disappointment, you have tormented me long enough, this is the end of your game, I shall see you no more, in the name of Jesus Christ.

17. Failure at the edge of breakthrough, you have tormented me long enough, this is the end of your game, I shall see you no more in the name of Jesus Christ.

18. O God my Father, let the Red Sea of this outgoing year take away my pain, in the name of Jesus Christ.

19. O God my Father, let the Red Sea of this outgoing year take away my sufferings, in the name of Jesus Christ.
20. O God my Father, let the Rea Sea of this outgoing year take away my failure, in the name of Jesus Christ.
21. Every opposition to my breakthroughs, go away and be wasted with this outgoing year, in the name of Jesus Christ.
22. O God my Father, let this outgoing year go away with all the problems she has brought into my life, in the name of Jesus Christ.
23. O God my Father, let this outgoing year go away with all the problems that I carried over from the previous years, in the name of Jesus Christ.
24. O God my Father, let your fire locate every hidden problem in my life and destroy it now, in the name of Jesus Christ.
25. O God my Father, let your fire locate every hidden agenda of the enemy designed to follow me into the New Year, destroy it now in the name of Jesus Christ.
26. Every evil mandate issued against me for the New Year, be destroyed by the fire of God in the name of Jesus Christ.
27. Every evil assignment given against me for the New Year, be cancelled now in the name of Jesus Christ.
28. Every satanic agent preparing to enter into the New Year to work against me, go away and perish with this outgoing year in the name of Jesus Christ.
29. Every problem designed to repeat itself in my life in the New Year, receive solution now in the name of Jesus Christ.
30. Every satanic warrant issued to arrest me in the New Year, be destroyed now, in the name of Jesus Christ.

31. Every agent of failure assigned to follow me into the New Year, you will not prosper, perish with this outgoing year in the name of Jesus Christ.

32. Every agent of fruitless hard-work assigned to follow me into the New Year, you will not prosper, perish with this outgoing year in the name of Jesus Christ.

33. Every agent of disappointment assigned to follow me into the New Year, you will not prosper, perish with this outgoing year in the name of Jesus Christ.

34. Every agent of backwardness assigned to follow me into the New Year, you will not prosper, perish with this outgoing year in the name of Jesus Christ.

35. Every agent of poverty assigned to follow me into the New Year, you will not prosper, perish with this outgoing year in the name of Jesus Christ.

36. Every agent of shame assigned to follow me into the New Year, you will not prosper, perish with this outgoing year in the name of Jesus Christ.

37. Every agent of demotion assigned to follow me into the New Year, you will not prosper, perish with this outgoing year in the name of Jesus Christ.

38. Every agent of confusion assigned to follow me into the New Year, you will not prosper, perish with this outgoing year in the name of Jesus Christ.

39. Every agent of misfortune assigned to follow me into the New Year, you will not prosper, perish with this outgoing year in the name of Jesus Christ.

40. Every agent of loneliness assigned to follow me into the New Year, you will not prosper, perish with this outgoing year, in the name of Jesus Christ.

41. Every agent of disgrace assigned to follow me into the New Year, you will not prosper, perish with this outgoing year in the name of Jesus Christ.

42. Every agent of rejection assigned to follow me into the New Year, you will not prosper, perish with this outgoing year in the name of Jesus Christ.

43. Every agent of limitation assigned to follow me into the New Year, you will not prosper, perish with this outgoing year in the name of Jesus Christ.

44. Every agent of demotion assigned to follow into the New Year, you will not prosper, perish with this outgoing year in the name of Jesus Christ.

45. Every agent of ridicule assigned to follow me into the New Year, you will not prosper, perish with this outgoing year in the name of Jesus Christ.

46. Household wickedness assigned to follow me into the New Year, you will not prosper, perish with this outgoing year in the name of Jesus Christ.

47. Every agent of infirmity assigned to follow me into the New Year, you will not prosper, perish with this outgoing year in the name of Jesus Christ.

48. Any power assigned to follow me into the New Year to hinder my prayers, you will not prosper, perish with this outgoing year in the name of Jesus Christ.

49. Any power planning to follow me into the New Year to delay my breakthroughs, you will not prosper, perish with this outgoing year in the name of Jesus Christ.

50. Any power planning to follow me into the New Year to frustrate my life, you will not prosper, perish with this outgoing year in the name of Jesus Christ.

51. Any power planning to follow me into the New Year to kill my dreams, you will not prosper, perish with this outgoing year in the name of Jesus Christ.
52. Any power planning to follow me into the New Year to enslave me, you will not prosper, perish with this outgoing year in the name of Jesus Christ.
53. Any power planning to follow into the New Year to attack my destiny, you will not prosper, perish with this outgoing year in the name of Jesus Christ.
54. Any power planning to follow me into the New Year to destroy my harvest, you will not prosper, perish with this outgoing year in the name of Jesus Christ.
55. Any power planning to follow me into the New Year to destroy my testimony, you will not prosper, perish with this outgoing year in the name of Jesus Christ.
56. Neighborhood wickedness planning to follow me into the New Year to trouble me, my God shall trouble today, perish with this outgoing year in the name of Jesus Christ.
57. Every serpentine spirit planning to follow me into the New Year, you will not prosper, perish with this outgoing year in the name of Jesus Christ.
58. Evil broadcasters planning to follow me into the New Year, you will not escape the judgment of God, perish with this outgoing year in the name of Jesus Christ.
59. Spirit of fear planning to follow me into the New Year, you will not prosper, loose your hold upon my life now in the name of Jesus Christ.
60. Agent of discouragement planning to follow me into the New Year, you will not prosper, perish with this outgoing year in the name of Jesus Christ.

61. Pharaoh of my father's house planning to follow me into the New Year, you will not prosper, perish with this outgoing year in the name of Jesus Christ.
62. Goliath of my father's house planning to follow me into the New Year, you will not prosper, perish with this outgoing year in the name of Jesus Christ.
63. Herod of my father's house planning to follow me into the New Year, you will not prosper, perish with this year in the name of Jesus Christ.
64. Ancestral problems that have been rolling with me from year to year, you are not allowed to follow me into the New Year, in the name of Jesus Christ.
65. Inherited failure that has been rolling with me from year to year, you are not allowed to follow me into the New Year, in the name of Jesus Christ.
66. Ancestral curses that have been rolling with me from year to year, you are not allowed to follow me into the New Year, in the name of Jesus Christ.
67. Foundational problems planning to follow me into the New Year, you will not prosper, perish with this outgoing year in the name of Jesus Christ.
68. Familiar spirit planning to follow me into the New Year, you will not prosper, perish with this outgoing year in the name of Jesus Christ.
69. Spirit of witchcraft planning to trouble me in the New Year, you will not prosper, perish with this outgoing year in the name of Jesus Christ.
70. Evil cycles that have been rolling with me from year to year, you are not allowed to follow me into the New Year, perish with this outgoing year in the name of Jesus Christ.

71. Spiritual robbers planning to follow me into the New Year, you will not prosper, perish with this outgoing year in the name of Jesus Christ.

72. Self-inflicted failure planning to follow me into the New Year, you will not prosper, perish with this outgoing year in the name of Jesus Christ.

73. Self-inflicted sickness planning to follow me into the New Year, you will not prosper, perish with this outgoing year in the name of Jesus Christ.

74. Satanic stronghold planning to follow me into the New Year, you will not prosper, perish with this outgoing year in the name of Jesus Christ.

75. Spirit of debt planning to follow me into the New Year, you will not prosper, perish with this outgoing year in the name of Jesus Christ.

76. Unrepentant enemies planning to follow me into the New Year, you will not prosper, perish with this outgoing year in the name of Jesus Christ.

77. Stubborn situations planning to follow me into the New Year, you will not prosper, perish with this outgoing year in the name of Jesus Christ.

78. Evil covenants planning to follow me into the New Year, be nullified now in the name of Jesus Christ.

79. Evil agreements planning to follow me into the New Year, be terminated now in the name of Jesus Christ.

80. Every satanic virus planning to follow me into the New Year, be destroyed by the fire of God in the name of Jesus Christ.

81. Spirit of deception planning to follow me into the New Year, be exposed and put to shame, perish with this outgoing year in the name of Jesus Christ.

82. Evil networks planning to follow me into the New Year, scatter by the fire of God and never to regroup again in the name of Jesus Christ.

83. People like Sanballat, Geshem and Tobiah planning to follow me into the New Year, O God my Father, put them to an open shame in the name of Jesus Christ.

84. People like Korah, Dathan and Abiram planning to follow me into the New Year, O earth open up your mouth and swallow them according to the Word of God in the name of Jesus Christ.

85. People like Achan planning to follow me into the New Year, my God will trouble you today in the name of Jesus Christ.

86. Spirit of Haman planning to follow me into the New Year, you will not prosper, perish with this outgoing year in the name of Jesus Christ.

87. Spirit of Sennacherib planning to follow me into the New Year, you will not prosper, perish with this outgoing year in the name of Jesus Christ.

88. Spirit of Saul planning to kill my David in the New Year, you will not prosper, perish with this outgoing year in the name of Jesus Christ.

89. Spirit of Pharaoh that refuses to let my Israel go, you will not prosper, perish with this outgoing year in the name of Jesus Christ.

90. Agent of barrenness planning to follow me into the New Year, you will not prosper, perish with this outgoing year in the name of Jesus Christ.

91. Spirit of devourer planning to follow me into the New Year, you will not prosper, perish with this outgoing year in the name of Jesus Christ.

92. Power of waster planning to follow me into the New Year, you will not prosper, perish with this outgoing year in the name of Jesus Christ.

93. Evil marks upon my life, be erased by the blood of Jesus Christ.

94. Spiritual ignorance planning to follow me into the New Year, you will not prosper, perish with this outgoing year in the name of Jesus Christ.

95. Desert spirit planning to follow me into the New Year, you will not prosper, perish with this outgoing year in the name of Jesus Christ.

96. Every satanic judgment against me, perish with this outgoing year in the name of Jesus Christ.

97. Every evil pronouncement against me, perish with this outgoing year in the name of Jesus Christ.

98. Every work of the devil in my life, perish with this outgoing year in the name of Jesus Christ.

99. Every attack of the enemy on my finances, perish with this outgoing year in the name of Jesus Christ.

DESTROYING THE WORKS OF THE DEVIL

Passages To Read Before You Pray:
1 John 3:8, Psalms 35, 59, 69, Revelation 12:11, Matthew 13:
24-30

PRAYER PONITS

1. Father Lord, I thank you because all power in heaven and on earth belongs to you.
2. Father Lord, I thank you for being on my side and no one can be against me.
3. Father Lord, forgive me of all my sins and cleanse me from all unrighteousness.
4. Father Lord, have mercy upon me and erase all my iniquities.
5. I cover myself and my household in the blood of Jesus.
6. I draw the bloodline to surround me and my household.
7. Every work of the devil in my life, be destroyed by fire.
8. Every work of the devil in my home, be destroyed by fire.
9. Every work of the devil in the life of my spouse, be destroyed by fire.
10. Every work of the devil in the life of my children, be destroyed by fire.
11. Every work of the devil in my marriage , be destroyed by fire.
12. Every work of the devil in my business, be destroyed by fire.
13. Every work of the devil manifesting in my finances, be destroyed by fire.

14. Every work of the devil against my destiny, be destroyed by fire.
15. Every work of the devil against my star, be destroyed by fire.
16. Every work of the devil against the plan of God for me, be destroyed by fire.
17. Every work of the devil against my future, be destroyed by fire.
18. Every work of the devil against my dream, be destroyed by fire.
19. Every work of the devil to hinder my progress, be destroyed by fire.
20. Every work of the devil to slow down my progress, be destroyed by fire.
21. Every work of the devil to reverse my progress, be destroyed by fire.
22. Every work of the devil to delay my miracles, be destroyed by fire.
23. Every work of the devil to rob me of my miracles, be destroyed by fire.
24. Every work of the devil to stop my miracles, be destroyed by fire.
25. Every work of the devil to make success impossible for me, be destroyed by fire.
26. Every work of the devil to delay my success, be destroyed by fire.
27. Every work of the devil to make my life miserable, be destroyed by fire.
28. Every work of the devil to rob me of my joy, be destroyed by fire.
29. Every work of the devil against my health, be destroyed by fire.

30. Every work of the devil manifesting in my body, be destroyed by fire.

31. Every work of the devil manifesting as hatred against me, be destroyed by fire.

32. Every work of the devil causing my life to go backward, be destroyed by fire.

33. Every work of the devil affecting my sources of income, be destroyed by fire.

34. Every work of the devil affecting my spiritual life , be destroyed by fire.

35. Every work of the devil affecting my prayer life, be destroyed by fire.

36. Every work of the devil affecting my relationship with God, be destroyed by fire.

37. Every work of the devil that puts my life on hold, be destroyed by fire.

38. Every work of the devil causing me to lose faith, be destroyed by fire.

39. Father Lord, let your spirit raise a stand against every work of the devil in my life.

40. Father Lord, let every work of the devil in my life be destroyed by the power in the blood of Jesus.

I SAY UNTO YOU, ARISE

Passages To Read Before You Pray:
Isaiah 61:1-11, Psalms 29, 32, 42, Mark 5:35-43

PRAYER PONITS

1. O God my father, I thank you for being my God.
2. O God my father, I thank you for the privilege to know you.
3. O God my father, I thank you because you always answer whenever I call upon you
4. On the basis of your mercy O Lord, forgive me of all my sins and wrong doings, in the name of Jesus.
5. I hereby cover myself in the precious blood of Jesus Christ.
6. I believe that my healing is made perfect, in the name of Jesus.
7. I believe that the power of God will set me free from any form of bondage.
8. I believe that my God will make a way for me where there seems to be no way.
9. I believe that the mighty hands of God will lift me up above every situation.
10. I believe that the mighty hands of God will bring a positive turn around into my life.
11. I hereby command my crippled blessings, arise and manifest in the name of Jesus Christ.
12. I hereby command my crippled business, arise and prosper in the name of Jesus Christ.

13. I say unto my hindered miracles, arise and manifest in the name of Jesus Christ.
14. I say unto my delayed promotion, arise and manifest in the name of Jesus Christ.
15. Today I say unto my troubled marriage, arise and experience the peace of God in the name of Jesus Christ.
16. Today I say unto my dead glory, arise and reflect the glory of God in the name of Jesus Christ.
17. Today I say unto every malfunctioned part of my body system, arise and function well in the name of Jesus Christ.
18. I hereby command my crippled finances, arise and show forth the glory of God in the name of Jesus Christ.
19. O God my father, let transformation begin in every area of my life, in the name of Jesus Christ.
20. O God my father, let transformation begin in my marriage, in the name of Jesus Christ.
21. O God my father, let transformation begin in the life of my husband/wife, in the name of Jesus Christ.
22. O God my father, let transformation begin in the life of my children, in the name of Jesus Christ.
23. O God my father, let transformation begin in my place of work, in the name of Jesus Christ.
24. O God my father, let transformation begin in my business, in the name of Jesus Christ.
25. O God my father, let transformation begin in my church, in the name of Jesus Christ.
26. O God my father, let transformation begin in my finances, in the name of Jesus Christ.
27. I receive the grace of God to do all good things that I have been unable to do, in the name of Jesus Christ.

28. I receive the grace of God to achieve great things that have been eluding me, in the name of Jesus Christ.
29. I receive the grace of God to fulfill purpose, in the name of Jesus Christ.
30. I receive the grace of God to fulfill destiny, in the name of Jesus Christ.
31. I receive the grace of God to move from the minimum to the maximum, in the name of Jesus Christ.
32. I receive the grace of God to overcome every obstacle confronting my breakthroughs in the name of Jesus Christ.
33. I receive the grace of God to overcome every hindrance that comes my way.
34. I receive the grace of God to overcome every challenge thrown at me.
35. O God my father, thank you for granting all my requests in the names of Jesus Christ.

I SHALL NOT BE FRUSTRATED

Passages To Read Before You Pray:
Psalms 2, 10, 13, 42, 105, 106

PRAYER POINTS

1. O God my father, I thank you for being my God.
2. O God my father, I thank you for the privilege to know you.
3. O God my father, I thank you because you always answer whenever I call upon you.
4. On the basis of your mercy O Lord, forgive me of all my sins and wrong doings, in the name of Jesus.
5. I hereby cover myself in the precious blood of Jesus Christ.
6. Any power, spirit or personality that receives assignments to frustrate me, be destroyed by fire.
7. Any power, spirit or personality that assigns anyone to frustrate me, be destroyed by fire.
8. I refuse to be frustrated in the name of Jesus Christ.
9. Any situation designed to frustrate me, receive solution.
10. Any circumstance created to frustrate me, receive solution.
11. I receive grace and power to overcome any form of frustration.
12. No matter what my enemies throw at me, I will not be frustrated.
13. Instead of frustration, I will be comforted.
14. Instead of frustration, I shall have joy everlasting.
15. Instead of frustration, I shall have the peace of God.

16. Any past mistakes that brings the fruit of frustration, be converted to miracles.
17. Every arrow of frustration shot at me, go back to your sender.
18. Every frustration that I created for myself ignorantly, receive solution now.
19. Touch me O Lord for a miracle.
20. Touch my situations O Lord, for unusual solutions.

I WILL NOT MISS MY MIRACLE

Passages To Read Before You Pray:
2 Kings 2:1-25, Psalms 34, 40, 78, Mark 5:25-34, 10:46-52

PRAYER PONITS

1. Father Lord, I thank you for your thoughts and plans for my life.
2. Father Lord, I thank you for being a caring father and a wonderful friend.
3. Forgive me , O Lord of any sin in my hands and any iniquity in my heart.
4. I cover myself and my household in the blood of Jesus.
5. O God my father, give me the grace to recognize the day of my blessing.
6. O God my father, give me the grace to recognize the time of my open heavens.
7. O God my father, give me the grace to recognize the moment of my breakthrough.
8. O God my father, give me boldness to confront and overcome every obstacle to my breakthrough.
9. O God my father, give me boldness to confront and overcome every obstacle to my miracles.
10. I refuse to listen to any voice discouraging me from moving forward.
11. I refuse to listen to any voice discouraging me from crossing my Jordan.
12. No matter the efforts of the enemies, I will not miss my blessing.

13. No matter the efforts of the enemies, I will not miss my miracles.
14. No matter the efforts of the enemies, I will not miss my breakthroughs.
15. No matter the efforts of the enemies, I will be in the right place at the right time.
16. Today O Lord, let me experience the demonstration of your power.
17. Every evil voice trying to convince me to act against the plan of God for me will not prosper.
18. Every evil voice trying to convince me to disobey the commandment of God will not prosper.
19. In the presence of those who are watching and laughing at me, O God my father decorate me with your glory.
20. In the presence of those who are watching and laughing at me, O God my father establish your kingdom in my life.
21. In the presence of those who are watching and laughing at me, O God my father promote me beyond the expectation of the enemies.
22. In the presence of those who are watching and laughing at me, O God my father fulfill your promises in my life.
23. In the presence of those who are watching and laughing at me, O God my father demonstrate your power in my life.
24. In the presence of those who are watching and laughing at me, O God my father bless me abundantly.
25. In the presence of those who are watching and laughing at me, O God my father give me the double portion of your power and anointing.
26. In the presence of those who are watching and laughing at me, O God my father multiply my harvest.

27. In the presence of those who are watching and laughing at me, O God my father release upon me the former rain.

28. In the presence of those who are watching and laughing at me, O God my father grant me unusual breakthroughs.

29. In the presence of those who are watching and laughing at me, O God my father crown me with the crown of glory.

30. In the presence of those who are watching and laughing at me, O God my father make me the head and not the tail.

31. In the presence of those who are watching and laughing at me, O God my father let all my dreams come to pass.

32. In the presence of those who are watching and laughing at me, O God my father let my life move forward.

33. In the presence of those who are watching and laughing at me, O God my father let my helpers locate me and help me.

34. In the presence of those who are watching and laughing at me, O God my father prosper the works of my hands.

LET THERE BE RESTORATION

Passages To Read Before You Pray:
Joel 2:18-26, Jeremiah 29:10-14, 33:14, Psalms 126

PRAYER POINTS

1. Father Lord, I thank you for your thoughts and plans for my life.
2. Father Lord, I thank you for being a caring father and a wonderful friend.
3. Forgive me, O Lord of any sin in my hands and any iniquity in my heart.
4. I cover myself and my household in the blood of Jesus.
5. Father Lord, let all my wasted time be restored back to me.
6. Father Lord, let all my wasted efforts be restored back to me.
7. Every unfulfilled promise of God for me, it is high time, come to fulfillment now.
8. Every unrealized goal, come to realization now.
9. Every unachieved desire, I receive the grace of God to achieve them.
10. Every lost opportunity, I claim it back.
11. Every lost blessing, I claim it back.
12. Every miracle designed for me that I have missed, I claim it back.
13. Every area that doors have been shut against me, let them be opened for me.
14. Every area that I have failed to fulfill purpose, I receive grace for a second chance.

15. All my mistakes, Lord, convert them to miracles.
16. All the good things the enemy has destroyed in my life, let them be restored to me.

MY DREAMS WILL NOT DIE

Passages To Read Before You Pray:
Genesis 37: 18-24, Ezekiel 37:1-11, Psalms 19, 29, 42, Jeremiah 29: 11

PRAYER POINTS

1. Father Lord, I thank you for your thoughts and plans for my life.
2. Father Lord, I thank you for being a caring father and a wonderful friend.
3. Forgive me, O Lord of any sin in my hands and any iniquity in my heart.
4. I cover myself and my household in the blood of Jesus.
5. I boldly declare, my dreams will not die.
6. Any power or principality trying to kill my dream, you will not prosper.
7. O God my Father, release blindness upon every evil eye monitoring my dreams.
8. I cover my dreams in the precious blood of Jesus.
9. Household wickedness trying to kill my dreams, you will not escape the judgment of God.
10. Every jealous friend trying to hinder or kill my dreams, you will not escape the judgment of God.
11. Every conspiracy against me because of my dreams, scatter by the fire of God.
12. Every conspiracy against my dreams, scatter by fire.
13. Every evil plot against me because of my dreams, scatter by the fire of God.

14. Every activity of the enemy against me because of my dreams, will not prosper.
15. Every activity of the enemy against my dreams will not prosper.
16. Anyone that wants to kill me because of my dreams, I command you to die before your time.
17. Any power that wants to kill me because of my dreams, I command you to die by the fire of God.
18. Household wickedness that wants to kill me because of my dreams, die by the fire of God.
19. Any principality that wants to kill my dreams before fulfillment, you will not escape the judgment of God.
20. Every satanic attack against me because of my dreams, go back to your sender.
21. Every demonic attack against my dreams, go back to the sender.
22. You agent of darkness, you cannot and will not kill my dreams.
23. Household wickedness, you cannot and will not kill my dreams.
24. Evil power of my father's house, you cannot and will not kill my dreams.
25. Witchcraft power, you cannot and will not kill my dreams.
26. Jealous members of my family, you cannot and will not kill my dreams.
27. I receive the grace of God to fulfill my dreams.
28. I receive the empowerment to fulfill my dreams.
29. I will not die before the fulfillment of my dreams.
30. O God my father, let my enemies witness the fulfillment of my dreams, so they may know that you are God.

31. Every effort of the enemy against me shall lead to the fulfillment of my dreams.
32. O God my Father, take me from the dream land to the land of fulfillment.
33. O God my Father, let everyone that mock my dreams witness the fulfillment.
34. O God my Father, let people who will contribute to the fulfillment of my dreams begin to locate me.
35. I cast down every evil imagination that rises against me because of my dreams.
36. I cast down every evil imagination that rises against my dreams.
37. Every evil network working to hinder my dreams, scatter.
38. Every evil network working to delay the fulfillment of my dreams, scatter.

MY LIFE WILL NOT BE A WASTE

Passages To Read Before You Pray:
Psalms 3, 9, 27, 109, 140, 1 Samuel 30:1-31

PRAYER POINTS

1. Father Lord, I thank you for the privilege to know you.
2. Father Lord, I thank you for the gift of life, and for sparing my life to see another day.
3. Father Lord, forgive me of any sin and any iniquity.
4. Any power assigned against me to waste my efforts, you will not escape the judgment of God.
5. Any power assigned to waste my blessings, you will not escape the judgment of God.
6. Any power assigned to waste my life, you must die.
7. Any power assigned to waste my appointed time, you will not escape the judgment of God.
8. You power of waster assigned against my finances, die by the fire of God.
9. You power of waster assigned against my destiny, die by the fire of God
10. You power of waster assigned against my dreams, you will not prosper.
11. You power of waster assigned against my marriage, you will not prosper.
12. You power of waster against my children, you will not prosper.
13. You power of waster assigned against my future, you will not prosper.

14. You power of waster assigned against my business, you will not prosper.
15. You power of waster assigned against every opportunity that comes my way, you will not prosper.
16. You power of waster assigned to waste my divine breakthroughs, you will not prosper.
17. You power of waster assigned against the works of my hands, you will not prosper.
18. You power of waster assigned to waste my relationships, you will not prosper.
19. You power of waster assigned to waste my progress, you will not escape the judgment of God.
20. My life will not be wasted; I cover my life in the blood of Jesus.

PRAYER AGAINST SATANIC DECREE

Passages To Read Before You Pray:
Esther 3: 8-15, Numbers 22, 23, 24, Isaiah 54, Psalm 69

PRAYER POINTS

1. O God my Father, I thank you for your Word is yes and amen, and your Word will surely come to pass in my life.
2. O God my Father, I thank you for the good things that you have started and you will perfect in my life in the name of Jesus Christ.
3. O God my Father, I thank you for always being there for me and with me in the name of Jesus Christ.
4. O God my Father, when I find myself in the time of trouble, when all hope is lost, thank you for being there for me.
5. Father Lord, I thank you for the privilege to know you.
6. Father Lord, I thank you for the gift of life, and for sparing my life to see another day.
7. Father Lord, on the basis of your mercy, forgive me of all my sins and cleanse me in the blood of Jesus Christ.
8. Every satanic warrant issued to arrest me, be cancelled.
9. Every satanic warrant issued to enslave me, be cancelled.
10. Every agent of hell dispatched to attack me, I send you back, go and destroy your sender.
11. Every agent of hell dispatched to destroy my harvest, be destroyed by the fire of God.

12. Every agent of hell dispatched to frustrate me, you are marked for destruction.
13. Every agent of hell released to delay my miracles, you are marked for destruction.
14. Every agent of hell released to hinder my progress, you are marked for destruction.
15. Every satanic network assigned to work on my case, be scattered by the fire of God.
16. Every satanic decree issued to terminate my life, be cancelled by fire.
17. Every satanic decree issued to make my life miserable, be cancelled.
18. Every satanic decree issued to keep me in bondage of fear, be destroyed.
19. Every agenda of darkness against my life be cancelled.
20. Every satanic crusade, you will not come near my household, I will not be your victim.

PRAYERS TO GET THE DESIRED JOB

Passages To Read Before You Pray:
2 Kings 6:1-7, 7:1-20, Psalms 23, 30, 42, 78

PRAYER POINTS

1. O God my Father, I thank you for your Word is yes and amen, and your Word will surely come to pass in my life.
2. O God my Father, I thank you for the good things that you have started and will perfect in my life in the name of Jesus Christ.
3. O God my Father, I thank you for always being there for me and with me in the name of Jesus Christ.
4. O God my Father, when I find myself in the time of trouble, when all hope is lost, thank you for being there for me.
5. Father Lord, on the basis of your mercy, forgive me of all my sins and cleanse me in the blood of Jesus Christ.
6. O God my Father, let the great door of opportunity to locate my desired job be opened unto me now in the name of Jesus Christ.
7. O God my Father, you are my present help in trouble, arise and help me to locate my desired job, I refuse to continue like this in the name of Jesus Christ.
8. Today O Lord, connect me to someone that will help me find a new and better job in the name of Jesus Christ.
9. O God my Father, let unusual favor be granted unto me wherever I have applied for employment in the name of Jesus Christ.

10. I cover myself in the precious blood of Jesus Christ.
11. I cover all my employment applications and resumes that I have submitted in the blood of Jesus Christ.
12. O God my Father, let my applications and resumes receive unusual favor in the sight of those that will make decision on whom to hire, in the name of Jesus Christ.
13. O God my Father, let the decision that the employer will make today favor me in every area, in the name of Jesus Christ.
14. I will not be rejected, wherever I have been turned for a job, Father Lord, let them call me back with a job offer in the name of Jesus Christ.
15. No matter the situation of the economy, O God my Father, I am a child of the Kingdom, arise and locate my job for me now in the name of Jesus Christ.
16. O God my Father, let the Holy Spirit guide me today to be in the right place at the right time in the name of Jesus Christ.
17. O God my Father, let the Holy Spirit lead me today to where my job is located in the name of Jesus Christ.
18. O God my Father, I refuse to continue like this, let there be a turnaround in my situation, in the name of Jesus Christ.
19. I have been chasing around a job for a while, it is high time O Lord, let my job locate me now in the name of Jesus Christ.
20. I hereby decree that those who have my employment application will go the extra miles to do me good and show me favor in the name of Jesus Christ.
21. I hereby decree that those who have my resume will put extra efforts to do me good and show me favor in the name of Jesus Christ.

22. O God my Father, I am ready to go to work, let the doors of opportunity be opened unto me now in the name of Jesus Christ.
23. O God my Father, I am ready to go to work, let every delay be removed now in the name of Jesus Christ.
24. O God my Father, I am ready to go to work, let every hindrance be removed now in the name of Jesus Christ.
25. O God my Father, I am ready to go to work, arise and locate my job now in the name of Jesus Christ.
26. O God my Father, let the Holy Spirit convince those who have my employment application to give me the opportunity and hire me in the name of Jesus Christ.
27. O God my Father, let the Holy Spirit convince those who have my resume to give me the opportunity and give me the job that I am praying for, in the name of Jesus Christ.
28. O God my Father, let my job come to me now in a miraculous way in the name of Jesus Christ.
29. O God my Father, let there be a miracle that will bring my job search to a glorious end, in the name of Jesus Christ.
30. I hereby decree that every situation around will begin to work for my good now and forever in the name of Jesus Christ.
31. O God my Father, let my status change now from unemployed to employed, in the name of Jesus Christ.
32. O God my Father, give me my desired job now, so that everyone around me may know that I serve a great God, in the name of Jesus Christ.
33. Today I decree that no matter the situation of the economy, it shall work for my good in the name of Jesus Christ.

34. O God my Father, bless me today with the job that will allow me to serve you in the name of Jesus Christ.

35. O God my Father, bless me today with the job that will not take me away from your presence in the name of Jesus Christ.

36. O God my Father, let the employers begin to call me with job offers in the name of Jesus Christ.

37. The time of drought in my life is over, the season of abundance has begun in the name of Jesus Christ.

38. The time of drought in my life is over, the season of plenty has begun in the name of Jesus Christ.

39. The time of drought in my life is over, the season of testimony has begun in the name of Jesus Christ.

40. The time of trial in my life is over, the season of celebration has begun in the name of Jesus Christ.

41. Thank you Father Lord for the answers to my prayers, and I will be careful to give you all the glory when my testimony comes, in the name of Jesus Christ I pray with much love and thanksgiving.

SHAPING YOUR CHILDREN'S FUTURE

Passages To Read Before You Pray:
Isaiah 8:18; 17:6-8; 54:13, 17; Psalm 1, 127, 128; Deuteronomy
28:2-13

PRAYER POINTS

1. O God my Father, I thank you for being a wonderful and a good God in my life and in my children's life.
2. O God my Father, I thank you for the wonderful children you have given me.
3. Lord, I thank you because you will fulfill all your plans and counsels concerning their lives.
4. I hereby cover my children in the precious blood of Jesus Christ.
5. No evil will come near my children, and no danger shall come near my dwelling place in the name of Jesus Christ.
6. My children are secured and protected in the name of the Lord Jesus which is a strong tower.
7. I keep my children under the shadow of the Almighty, in the secret place of the Most High in the name of Jesus Christ.
8. No weapon that is formed against my children will prosper, in the name of Jesus Christ.
9. Every tongue that rises against my children is condemned according to the Word of God, in the name of Jesus Christ.
10. Anything that I have done that may affect my children or give the enemy access to their lives, Father Lord, forgive

me today on the basis of your mercy and cleanse me in the blood of Jesus Christ.

11. By the authority and power in the name of Jesus Christ, my children shall be for signs and wonders in their father's house, in the name of Jesus Christ.

12. By the authority and power in the name of Jesus Christ, my children shall be for signs and wonders among their friends and family, in the name of Jesus Christ.

13. By the authority and power in the name of Jesus Christ, my children shall be for signs and wonders in their schools and places of study, in the name of Jesus Christ.

14. By the authority and power in the name of Jesus Christ, my children shall be for signs and wonders in their place of work and among their colleagues, in the name of Jesus Christ.

15. By the authority and power in the name of Jesus Christ, my children shall be for signs and wonders in their place of birth in the name of Jesus Christ.

16. By the authority and power in the name of Jesus Christ, my children shall be for signs and wonders in this nation and in the nations of the world in the name of Jesus Christ.

17. By the authority and power in the name of Jesus Christ, my children shall be for signs and wonders in the earth, in the name of Jesus Christ.

18. My children shall be taught of the Lord and be full of wisdom all the days of their lives in the name of Jesus Christ.

19. My children shall be taught of the Lord and be full of knowledge and understanding all the days of their lives, in the name of Jesus Christ.

20. I decree great peace into the life of my children in every day of their lives, in the name of Jesus Christ.

21. I decree great peace into my children's academic life, in the name of Jesus Christ.

22. I decree great peace into my children's marital life, in the name of Jesus Christ.

23. I decree great peace into my children's businesses, in the name of Jesus Christ.

24. I decree great peace into every area of my children's life, in the name of Jesus Christ.

25. As from this day, my children shall reflect the glory of God in every area of their lives and in whatsoever they do and wherever they may find themselves, in the name of Jesus Christ.

26. O God my Father, let the nations of the world be blessed through my children, in the name of Jesus Christ.

27. By the authority and power in the name of Jesus Christ, my children shall be mighty on the earth, in the name of Jesus Christ.

28. By the authority and power in the name of Jesus Christ, my children shall give me joy in every day of their lives, in the name of Jesus Christ.

29. By the authority and power in the name of Jesus Christ, my children shall never be put to shame.

30. By the authority and power in the name of Jesus Christ, my children shall possess the gates of their enemies.

31. By the authority and power in the name of Jesus Christ, it shall be well with my children in every area of their lives.

32. It shall be well with my children in their academics, in the name of Jesus Christ.

33. It shall be well with my children in their marriages, in the name of Jesus Christ.
34. It shall be well with my children in their businesses, in the name of Jesus Christ.
35. It shall be well with my children in their careers, in the name of Jesus Christ.
36. It shall be well with my children in whatsoever they do and wherever they may find themselves, in the name of Jesus Christ.
37. My children shall be like a Olive tree around my table, in the name of Jesus Christ.
38. The goodness and mercies of God will follow my children and be their portions all the days of their life, in the name of Jesus Christ.
39. My children shall be like a tree planted by the rivers of water that brings forth fruits in its season, in the name of Jesus Christ.
40. My children shall prosper in whatsoever they do, in the name of Jesus Christ.
41. O God my Father, let the grace to do your will rest upon my children now and forever, in the name of Jesus Christ.
42. O God my Father, let the grace to obey you at all times rest upon my children now and forever, in the name of Jesus Christ.
43. O God my Father, let the grace to worship and serve you rest upon my children now and forever, in the name of Jesus Christ.
44. Today I decree that my children shall be lifted above their peers in every area of their academics, in the name of Jesus Christ.

45. Today I decree that my children shall be lifted above their peers in their workplaces, in the name of Jesus Christ.
46. Today I decree that my children shall be lifted above their peers in their businesses, in the name of Jesus Christ.
47. Today I decree that my children shall be lifted above their peers among family and friends, in the name of Jesus Christ.
48. Today I decree that my children shall be lifted above their peers in this nation and the nations around the world, in the name of Jesus Christ.
49. My children shall be blessed with the blessings of heaven above according to the Word of God, in the name of Jesus Christ.
50. My children shall be blessed with the blessings of the deep that lie under according to the Word of God, in the name of Jesus Christ.
51. My children shall be blessed with the blessings of the womb according to the Word of God, in the name of Jesus Christ.
52. My children shall be blessed with the blessings of the breasts according to the Word of God, in the name of Jesus Christ.
53. O God my Father, let my children be blessed in their fields beyond human comprehension, in the name of Jesus Christ.
54. O God my Father, let there be increase in every area of the life of my children that the world may know that I serve a good God, in the name of Jesus Christ.
55. O God my Father, let my children be established in every good works in the name of Jesus Christ.

56. O God my Father, command your blessings upon the finances and the life of my children, in the name of Jesus Christ.

57. O God my Father, open your good treasure unto my children and make them to be prosperous in whatsoever they do, in the name of Jesus Christ.

58. O God my Father, let the former and the latter rain be released upon my children, upon their seeds, fields and harvest, in the name of Jesus Christ.

59. My children shall be the head and not the tail, in the name of Jesus Christ.

60. My children shall be the leader and not the follower, in the name of Jesus Christ.

61. The grace of God and the anointing to fulfill purpose, rest upon my children now and forever, in the name of Jesus Christ.

62. My children shall wax great in life until they become very great, in the name of Jesus Christ.

63. The greatness of my children shall have no limit, in the name of Jesus Christ.

64. My children shall be above only and not be beneath, in the name of Jesus Christ.

65. My children shall be a blessing to their generation and generations to come, in the name of Jesus Christ.

66. O God my Father let the Spirit of excellence dwell in the life of my children from now and forever more, in the name of Jesus Christ.

67. Today I decree that my children's names shall be on the top of the list of great people of the world, in the name of Jesus Christ.

68. Today I decree that my children's names shall be on the top of the list of the richest and wealthiest people of the world, in the name of Jesus Christ.

69. Today I decree that my children's names shall be on the top of the list of the most influential people of the world, in the name of Jesus Christ.

70. O God my Father, connect my children to the people that will lead them to the top, in the name of Jesus Christ.

71. O God my Father, connect my children to the people that you have chosen to help them, in the name of Jesus Christ.

72. Today I decree that my children shall be the lender and not the borrower, in the name of Jesus Christ.

73. Today I decree that my children shall lend unto many nations, in the name of Jesus Christ.

74. Today I decree that my children will stand out in whatsoever they do and wherever they may find themselves, in the name of Jesus Christ.

75. O God my Father, let the anointing for fruitfulness rest upon my children now and forever, in the name of Jesus Christ.

76. O God my Father, let the anointing for increase rest upon my children now and forever, in the name of Jesus Christ.

77. O God my Father, let the anointing for abundance rest upon my children now and forever, in the name of Jesus Christ.

78. O God my Father, let the anointing for prosperity rest upon my children now and forever, in the name of Jesus Christ.

79. O God my Father, make my children exceedingly fruitful in every area of their life, in the name of Jesus Christ.
80. O God my Father, establish your everlasting covenant between you and my children now and forever, in the name of Jesus Christ.
81. Today I decree that my children will never lack any good thing all the days of their life, in the name of Jesus Christ.
82. Today I decree that my children shall be greater than their parents and everyone around them, in the name of Jesus Christ.

LORD, DEMONSTRATE YOUR POWER

Passages To Read Before You Pray:
Joshua1:1-18, Deuteronomy 11: 25, Ezekiel

PRAYER PONITS

1. O God my Father, I thank you for your Word is yes and amen, and your Word will surely come to pass in my life.
2. O God my Father, I thank you for the good things that you have started in my life and you will perfect it in the name of Jesus Christ.
3. O God my Father, I thank you for always being there for me and with me in the name of Jesus Christ.
4. O God my Father, when I find myself in the time of trouble, when all hope is lost, thank you for being there for me.
5. Father Lord, on the basis of your mercy, forgive me of all my sins and cleanse me in the blood of Jesus Christ.
6. I receive unstoppable miracles in the name of Jesus Christ.
7. I receive undeniable blessings in the name of Jesus Christ.
8. I shall have unstoppable achievements in the name of Jesus Christ.
9. I am moving forward and I cannot be stopped because God is with me.
10. I receive undeniable promotion in the name of Jesus Christ.
11. O God my Father, turn my tears to joy and celebration.

12. O God my Father, turn my delay to dancing.
13. O God my Father, turn my test to testimony.
14. O God my Father, turn my disappointment into a worldwide celebration.
15. O God my Father, let every hidden place of the enemy in my life be exposed and destroyed.
16. O God my Father, let every hidden place of the enemy in my family be exposed and destroyed.
17. O God my Father, let every hidden place of the enemy in my father's house be exposed and destroyed.
18. O God my Father, let every hidden place of the enemy in my finances be exposed and destroyed.
19. O God my Father, let every hidden place of the enemy in my house be exposed and destroyed.
20. O God my Father, let every hidden place of the enemy in my neighborhood be exposed and destroyed.
21. O God my Father, release the healing anointing upon me.
22. O God my Father, release the healing anointing upon my family.
23. O God my Father, release the healing anointing upon everyone that is sick around me.
24. O God my Father, whatever must be removed in my life for me to receive my miracles, let it be removed now.
25. O God my Father, whatever must be removed in my life for me to have breakthroughs, let it be removed now.
26. O God my Father, whatever must be removed in my life for me to move forward, let it be removed now.
27. O God my Father, whatever must be removed in my life for me to have financial freedom, let it be removed now.
28. O God my Father, whatever must die for me to see your glory, let it die by your fire.

29. O God my Father, whatever must die for me to live a life that pleases you, let it die by your fire.
30. O God my Father, move me from where I am to where you designed for me to be.
31. Anything programmed in my foundation to waste my destiny, be destroyed by the fire of God.
32. Anything programmed in my foundation to delay my progress in life, be destroyed by the fire of God.
33. Anything programmed in my foundation to keep me in bondage, be destroyed by the fire of God.
34. Anything programmed in my foundation to keep my helpers away from me, be destroyed by the fire of God.
35. Anything programmed in my foundation that attracts failure, be destroyed by the fire of God.
36. Anything programmed in my foundation that attracts poverty, be destroyed by the fire of God.
37. Anything programmed in my foundation that attracts problems, be destroyed by the fire of God.
38. Anything programmed in my foundation causing me to fail at the edge of breakthrough, be destroyed by fire.
39. Anything programmed in my foundation causing my life to go backwards, be destroyed by the fire of God.
40. Anything programmed in my foundation causing my life to be stagnant, be destroyed by the fire of God.
41. Anything programmed in my foundation attracting shame, be destroyed by the fire of God.
42. Anything programmed in my foundation attracting ridicule, be destroyed by the fire of God.
43. O God my Father, heal my foundation.
44. O God my Father, release your fire to purge my foundation.
45. O God my Father, let your fire consume anything that is not of God in my foundation.

O GOD ARISE AND ATTEND TO MY CASE

Passages To Read Before You Pray:
Judges 5: 31, Psalm 68, 74, Deuteronomy 32: 39-42, Exodus
15:6

PRAYER POINTS

1. O God my Father, I thank you for your Word is yes and amen, and your Word will surely come to pass in my life.
2. O God my Father, I thank you for the good things you have started in my life and that you will perfect it in the name of Jesus Christ.
3. O God my Father, I thank you for always being there for me and with me in the name of Jesus Christ.
4. O God my Father, when I find myself in the time of trouble, when all hope is lost, thank you for being there for me.
5. Father Lord, on the basis of your mercy, forgive me of all my sins and cleanse me in the blood of Jesus Christ.
6. O God my Father, arise and stop the wasters determined to waste my resources.
7. O God my Father, arise and stop the wasters determined to waste my destiny.
8. O God my Father, arise and stop the wasters determined to waste my efforts.
9. O God my Father, arise and stop the wasters determined to waste my blessings.
10. O God my Father, arise and stop the wasters determined to waste my time and life.

11. O God my Father, arise and destroy the power determined to hinder my prayers.
12. O God my Father, arise and destroy any power determined to hinder my miracles.
13. O God my Father, arise and destroy any power challenging your power in my life.
14. O God my Father, arise and destroy any power determined to stop my progress.
15. O God my Father, arise and destroy any power assigned to frustrate me.
16. O God my Father, arise and scatter every evil gathering set up against me.
17. O God my Father, arise and destroy the devourer attacking my finances.
18. O God my Father, arise and destroy any power assigned to make my life miserable.
19. O God my Father, arise and destroy any power determined to spoil my joy.
20. O God my Father, arise and destroy any power determined to hinder my breakthroughs.
21. O God my Father, arise and destroy any power determined to steal my harvest.
22. O God my Father, arise and destroy any power determined to destroy my harvest.
23. O God my Father, arise and destroy any power determined to shut my heavens.
24. O God my Father, arise and disgrace every agent of shame working against me.
25. O God my Father, arise and disgrace every agent of failure working against me.
26. O God my Father, arise and arrest the spirit of stagnancy manifesting in my life.

27. O God my Father, arise and arrest the spirit of stagnancy manifesting in my business.
28. O God my Father, arise and deliver me from the spirit of confusion working against me.
29. O God my Father, arise and deliver me from the spirit of fear holding me captive.
30. O God my Father, arise and deliver me from the hands of the taskmaster working against me.
31. O God my Father, arise and move me forward by fire.
32. O God my Father, arise and prosper the works of my hands.
33. O God my Father, arise and promote me in every area.
34. O God my Father, arise and scatter every wicked agenda against my life.
35. O God my Father, arise and destroy every activity of the enemy against my life.

DELIVER ME FROM MY STUBBORN ENEMY

Passages To Read Before You Pray:
Psalms 3, 9, 35, 55, 59, 69, 70

PRAYER PONITS

1. O God my Father, I thank you for your Word is yes and amen, and your Word will surely come to pass in my life.
2. O God my Father, I thank you for the good things that you have started in my life and you will perfect it in the name of Jesus Christ.
3. O God my Father, I thank you for always being there for me and with me in the name of Jesus Christ.
4. O God my Father, when I find myself in the time of trouble, when all hope is lost, thank you for being there for me.
5. Father Lord, on the basis of your mercy, forgive me of all my sins and cleanse me in the blood of Jesus Christ.
6. O God my Father, take not your hands from my life.
7. O God my Father, uproot depression and low self-esteem.
8. O God my Father, let there be solution to any issue affecting my peace.
9. O God my Father, I need a miracle now before the end of this prayer session.
10. O God my Father, do at last what the enemy says cannot be done in my life.

11. Before I finish this prayer session, Father Lord, let all my worries and fears disappear.
12. O God my Father, let the bitter water in my life dry up by your fire.
13. O God my Father, turn every desert point of my life into an oasis.
14. Today I bind depression and cast it out of my life.
15. Today I bind self-pity and cast it out of my life.
16. Lord, make a way for me where there seems to be no way.
17. Father, let great and mighty things begin to manifest in my life.
18. With God on my side, I will laugh last.
19. O Lord, give me a new laugh.
20. O God my Father, give me a new dance.
21. O Lord, deliver my family from the hands of stubborn enemies.
22. O Lord, deliver my business from the hands of stubborn enemies.
23. O Lord, deliver my church and church family from the hands of stubborn enemies.
24. O Lord, deliver my helpers from the hands of stubborn enemies.
25. O Lord, deliver my finances from the hands of stubborn enemies.
26. O Lord, deliver my destiny from the hands of stubborn enemies.
27. O Lord, deliver my dreams from the hands of stubborn enemies.
28. O Lord, deliver my breakthroughs from the hands of stubborn enemies.

29. O Lord, deliver my miracles from the hands of stubborn enemies.
30. O Lord, deliver my future from the hands of stubborn enemies.
31. O God my Father, let all the plans of my enemies be disappointed.
32. From today onward, my enemies shall bow to me.
33. O Lord, deliver my glory from the hands of stubborn enemies.
34. O Lord, deliver my joy from the hands of stubborn enemies.
35. O Lord, deliver my money from the hands stubborn enemies.
36. O Lord, deliver my promotion from the hands of stubborn enemies.
37. O Lord, deliver my freedom from the hands of stubborn enemies.
38. O Lord, deliver my testimony from the hands of stubborn enemies.
39. O Lord, deliver my celebration from the hands of stubborn enemies.
40. Every day of this year from the beginning to the end will favor me.

FATHER, LIFT UP A STANDARD

Passages To Read Before You Pray:
Isaiah 41:10-13, 54:1-17, 59:1-21, Psalms 2, 9, 60

PRAYER PONITS

1. O God my Father, I thank you for your Word is yes and amen, and your Word will surely come to pass in my life.
2. O God my Father, I thank you for the good things that you have started in my life and you will perfect it in the name of Jesus Christ.
3. O God my Father, I thank you for always being there for me and with me in the name of Jesus Christ.
4. O God my Father, when I find myself in the time of trouble, when all hope is lost, thank you for being there for me.
5. Father Lord, on the basis of your mercy, forgive me of all my sins and cleanse me in the blood of Jesus Christ.
6. O God my father, let the tempest and storm of my life hear your voice and disappear.
7. O God my father, the wind and sea obey you, because you live in me I command the storm of my life to give way for peace and calmness.
8. O Lord, let every evil plan fashioned against my life be disappointed.
9. O Lord, let every evil plan fashioned against my family be disappointed.
10. O Lord, let every evil plan fashioned against my church be disappointed.
11. O Lord, let every evil plan fashioned against my business or career be disappointed.

12. Miracles will happen in my life, I don't know how you will do it O Lord, but I know I will not be ashamed.
13. O God my father, contend with whatever is making you a liar in my life.
14. O God my father, contend with whatever is making you a liar in my church.
15. O God my father, contend with whatever is making you a liar in my finances.
16. O God my father, contend with whatever is making you a liar concerning your promises for me.
17. O Lord, give me the grace to trust you with all my heart.
18. O God my father, lift up a standard against every enemy of my life.
19. O God my father, lift up a standard against every enemy of my success.
20. O God my father, lift up a standard against every enemy of my marriage.
21. O God my father, lift up a standard against every enemy of my church and church family.
22. O God my father, lift up a standard against every enemy of my breakthroughs.
23. O God my father, give me the grace and the anointing to overcome every trial and challenge that is confronting me.
24. I receive the grace and the anointing to overcome every trial and challenge that is confronting my finances.
25. I receive the grace and the anointing to overcome every trial and challenge that is confronting my family.
26. I receive the grace and the anointing to overcome every trial and challenge that is confronting my marriage.
27. No matter what the enemies are doing around me, my life will not be affected.

28. No matter what the enemies are doing around me, my house will not be affected.
29. No matter what the enemies are doing around me, my finances will not be affected.
30. No matter what the enemies are doing around me, my destiny will not be affected.
31. No matter what the enemies are doing around me, my business or career will not be affected.
32. O God my father, intervene in this matter that is challenging your power in my life.
33. Every evil mark stamped on my life, I command you to be broken.
34. Every evil mark stamped on my marriage, I command you to be broken.
35. Every evil mark stamped on my church, I command you to be broken.
36. Every evil mark stamped on my destiny, I command you to be broken.
37. O God my father, let every power planning to put off the light of my destiny be disappointed.
38. O God my father, let every power planning to put off the light of my ministry be disappointed.

THE COUNSEL OF GOD ALONE SHALL STAND

Passages To Read Before You Pray:
2 Samuel 15:1-37, Psalms 17, 46, 138, Philippians 1:6

PRAYER POINTS

1. O God my Father, I thank you for your Word is yes and amen, and your Word will surely come to pass in my life.
2. O God my Father, I thank you for the good things that you have started in my life and you will perfect it in the name of Jesus Christ.
3. O God my Father, I thank you for always being there for me and with me in the name of Jesus Christ.
4. O God my Father, when I find myself in the time of trouble, when all hope is lost, thank you for being there for me.
5. Father Lord, on the basis of your mercy, forgive me of all my sins and cleanse me in the blood of Jesus Christ.
6. I might not know why I go through what am going through, but O Lord, perfect your good work in my family.
7. I might not understand why my family suffer this much, but O Lord, perfect your good work in my family.
8. I might not understand why my finances suffer this much, but O Lord, perfect your good work in my finances.
9. O God my father, repair and shake my foundation and enable it to carry your great plans.
10. O God my father, you are the distributer of riches and wealth, remember me and give me my share.

11. I cut off every evil link with my past.
12. O God my father, have mercy and deliver me from the fruits of the wrong things that I have done in the past.
13. O God my Father, no matter the situation, do not allow me to fail in the school of life.
14. O God my Father, you cannot lie, give me an expected end as you promised, give me a better tomorrow.
15. O God my Father, let your counsel alone stand concerning my life.
16. O God my Father, let your counsel alone stand concerning this ministry.
17. O God my Father, let your counsel alone stand concerning my marriage.
18. O God my Father, let your counsel alone stand concerning my destiny.
19. O God my Father, let the counsel of Ahitophel concerning my life be disappointed.
20. O God my Father, let the counsel of Ahitophel concerning my destiny be disappointed.
21. O God my Father, let the counsel of Ahitophel concerning my family be disappointed.
22. O God my Father, let the counsel of Ahitophel concerning my finances be disappointed.
23. O God my Father, let the counsel of Ahitophel concerning my breakthroughs be disappointed.
24. I shall not fear, no evil shall prevail against me.
25. I shall not fear, no evil shall prevail against my family.
26. I shall not fear, no evil shall prevail against my marriage.
27. I shall not fear, no evil shall prevail against my church and church family.
28. I shall not fear, no evil shall prevail against my finances.
29. I shall not fear, no evil shall prevail against my helpers.

30. O God my Father, have mercy upon me and disgrace the evil boasting of my enemies.
31. Satan, you are a liar, your plans to embarrass me will not stand, I command your plan to scatter.
32. Satan, you are a liar, your plan to delay my miracles will not stand, I command your plan to scatter.
33. Satan, you are a liar, your plan to hinder my blessings will not stand, I command your plan to scatter.
34. Satan, you are a liar, your plan to kill my dreams will not stand, I command your plan to scatter.
35. Satan, you are a liar, your plan to frustrate me will not stand, I command your plan to scatter.
36. Satan, you are a liar, your plan to hinder my prayers will not stand, I command your plan to scatter.
37. O God my Father, shake up my relationship and everyone around me, remove anyone that is affecting my growth and progress.
38. I command every arrow of pain and frustration to return back to the sender now.
39. I command every arrow of failure and stagnation to return back to the sender now.
40. O God my Father, crown my head with honor, I shall not end this prayer program in shame.

COURAGE TO CONFRONT AND CONQUER

Passages To Read Before You Pray:
Nehemiah 4: 1-23, 1 Samuel 17:1-58, Psalms 27, 118

PRAYER POINTS

1. O God my Father, I thank you for your Word is yes and amen, and your Word will surely come to pass in my life.
2. O God my Father, I thank you for the good things that you have started in my life and you will perfect it in the name of Jesus Christ.
3. O God my Father, I thank you for always being there for me and with me in the name of Jesus Christ.
4. O God my Father, when I find myself in the time of trouble, when all hope is lost, thank you for being there for me.
5. Father Lord, on the basis of your mercy, forgive me of all my sins and cleanse me in the blood of Jesus Christ.
6. O God my Father, let the counsel of Sanballat, Geshem, and Tobiah against my life be disappointed.
7. O God my Father, let the counsel of Sanballat, Geshem, and Tobiah against my marriage be disappointed.
8. O God my Father, let the counsel of Sanballat, Geshem, and Tobiah against my dream be disappointed.
9. O God my Father, let the counsel of Sanballat, Geshem, and Tobiah against my household be disappointed.
10. No matter the effort of my enemies, I will not give up.
11. No matter the effort of my enemies, I will not lose hope.
12. No matter the effort of my enemies, I will not be discouraged.

13. O God my Father, let Sanballat, Geshem, and Tobiah around me be put to an open shame.
14. You Sanballat, Geshem, and Tobiah trying to hinder what God is doing in my life, you will not escape the judgment of God.
15. You Sanballat, Geshem, and Tobiah trying to hinder what God is doing in my business, you will not escape the judgment of God.
16. You Sanballat, Geshem, and Tobiah trying to hinder what God is doing in my household, you will not escape the judgment of God.
17. You Sanballat, Geshem, and Tobiah trying to hinder what God is doing in my church, you will escape the judgment of God.
18. No matter the efforts of my enemies, my arms will be strengthened.
19. O God my Father, grant me wisdom to know which battles I must ignore and which ones I must face and fight.
20. O God my Father, give me courage to confront and overcome what I must confront to breakthrough in life.
21. O God my Father, give me courage to confront and overcome what I must confront to get to the top of the ladder.
22. O God my Father, give me courage to confront and overcome what I must confront to enter into my promise land.
23. O God my Father, give me courage to confront and overcome what I must confront to receive my promotion.

24. O God my Father, give me courage to confront and overcome what I must confront to receive total deliverance.
25. O God my Father, give me courage to confront and overcome what I must confront to receive financial freedom.
26. I am on the way to achieve my goal, I reject every satanic distraction.
27. I am on the way to fulfill my dreams, I reject every satanic distraction.
28. As I call forth my promotion to manifest, I refuse to be distracted.
29. As I call forth my miracles to manifest, I refuse to be distracted.
30. As I call forth my breakthroughs to manifest, I refuse to be distracted.
31. As I call forth my helpers to locate me, I refuse to be distracted.
32. As I am full of expectation to receive answers to my prayers, I refuse to be distracted.
33. As I lift up my hands and open my heart to fellowship with God, I refuse to be distracted.
34. O God my Father, use whatever I have, to take me to wherever I was created to reach.
35. I receive the anointing and the power to possess the gates of my enemies.
36. I receive the anointing and power to possess my possessions.
37. I will see and enjoy the goodness of the Lord in the land of the living.
38. O God my Father, I refuse to give up, show your greatness in my life.

39. O God my Father, I refuse to give up, show your greatness in my home.
40. O God my Father, I refuse to give up, show your greatness in this ministry.
41. O God my Father, I refuse to give up, show your greatness in my finances.
42. I reject the lie of the devil, it is not over for me, this is the beginning of my success.
43. I reject the lie of the devil, it is not over for me, this is the beginning of my greatness.
44. I reject the lie of the devil, it is not over for me, I will overcome this situation and testify.
45. O God my Father, help me trust you even when things are not going as expected.
46. I cast away doubt and unbelief, I am trusting God afresh for the miraculous, though it looks ridiculous.
47. I choose to walk by faith and not by sight.

SHOW ME YOUR FAITHFULNESS

Passages To Read Before You Pray:
Isaiah 8:18, Psalms 19, 29, 100, 136, 119:89-96

PRAYER POINTS

1. O God my Father, I thank you for your Word is yes and amen, and your Word will surely come to pass in my life.
2. O God my Father, I thank you for the good things that you have started in my life and you will perfect it in the name of Jesus Christ.
3. O God my Father, I thank you for always being there for me and with me in the name of Jesus Christ.
4. O God my Father, when I find myself in the time of trouble, when all hope is lost, thank you for being there for me.
5. Father Lord, on the basis of your mercy, forgive me of all my sins and cleanse me in the blood of Jesus Christ.
6. O God my Father, show your faithfulness unto my family from now and forever more.
7. O God my Father, show your faithfulness unto me from now and forever more.
8. O God my Father, show your faithfulness in every area of my interest from now and forever more.
9. O God my Father, use my life to show the world that indeed you are a faithful God.
10. O God my Father, use my marriage to show the world that indeed you are a faithful God.

11. O God my Father, use my business to show the world that indeed you are a faithful God.
12. O God my Father, use my finances to show the world that indeed you are a faithful God.
13. O God my Father, use my children to show the world that indeed you are a faithful God.
14. O God my Father, use my situation to show the world that indeed you are a faithful God.
15. O God my Father, grant me a tangible celebration before the end of this prayer program.
16. O God my Father, grant me the grace to trust you and never waver.
17. O God my Father, use my life to show that out of nothing, as in the beginning, can grow out beauty.
18. O God my Father, use my family to show that out of nothing, as in the beginning, can grow out beauty.
19. O God my Father, use my ministry to show you are the mighty God that can do anything.
20. O God my Father, use my finances to show that you are a mighty God, and nothing is impossible with you.
21. O God my Father, decorate my life with your glory.
22. O God my Father, turn my failures to fortunes.
23. O God my Father, turn my wounds to wisdom.
24. O God my Father, I refuse to depend on my ability for success.
25. O God my Father, give me power to get wealth according to your word.
26. I depend on your mercy O Lord, for breakthroughs in every area of my life.
27. O God my Father, when I think I am a failure, remind me that your mercies are sure.

28. I render useless every plan of Balaam to make me sin against God.
29. I receive the grace of God to end well whatsoever I lay my hands on.
30. I receive the grace of God to receive my miracles.
31. O God my Father, you can do all things, you can change destinies, change my story for the better.
32. O God my Father, grant me 24 hour miracles as you did in Samaria in the days of Elisha the prophet.
33. O God my Father, let every battle of life lead me to my Promise Land.
34. O God my Father, deliver me from any secret trap that has been programmed to put me in trouble.
35. O God my Father, let every plan to bring me to shame be disappointed.
36. O God my Father, let every plan of the enemy designed to bring me demotion be disappointed.
37. O God my Father, let every plan of the enemy designed to ridicule me be disappointed.
38. O God my Father, stir me up and take me to my Promise Land.
39. My best is yet to come, I shall not end as a failure.
40. O God my Father, give me the grace to make the best use of each day of this year.
41. O God my Father, disappoint any power that wants to make you a liar concerning my life.
42. O God my Father, disappoint any power that wants to make you a liar concerning my family.
43. O God my Father, disappoint any power that wants to make you a liar concerning my destiny.
44. O God my Father, disappoint any power that wants to make you a liar concerning my ministry.

45. O God my Father, contend with them that are contending with your glory in my life.
46. O God my Father, let my stubborn enemies go the way of Jezebel.
47. O God my Father, restore back unto me all that I have lost this year due to procrastination.
48. O God my Father, let my roaming blessings locate me now.
49. O God my Father, show me your glory as you did unto Isaiah and Moses.
50. O God of Joseph, grant me the grace to forget all my sorrow.
51. O God my Father, grant me the grace to forget all my pain.
52. O God my Father, let Satan's defeat in heaven and on the cross be evident in my life.
53. Every dragon warring against my destiny, you will not escape the judgment of God.
54. By the blood of Jesus Christ, I pronounce the disgrace of the devil and his agents concerning my life.
55. O God of Father, help me never to forget your goodness and mercy in my life.

HELP ME LORD, TO PUT MY LIFE IN ORDER

Passages To Read Before You Pray:
Genesis 1:1-5, Luke 8:22-25, Psalms 42, 46, 86

PRAYER POINTS

1. O God my Father, I thank you for your Word is yes and amen, and your Word will surely come to pass in my life.
2. O God my Father, I thank you for the good things that you have started in my life and you will perfect in the name of Jesus Christ.
3. O God my Father, I thank you for always being there for me and with me in the name of Jesus Christ.
4. O God my Father, when I find myself in the time of trouble, when all hope is lost, thank you for being there for me.
5. Father Lord, on the basis of your mercy, forgive me of all my sins and cleanse me in the blood of Jesus Christ.
6. O God my Father, help me to put my life in order.
7. Every chaotic situation in my life, receive solution now.
8. O God my Father, let the emptiness in my life be filled your presence and glory.
9. I shall not die before my God-appointed time.
10. I shall live to fulfill purpose and destiny.
11. You spirit of procrastination, I bind you and cast you out of my life, you are no longer allowed to rob me of my blessings.
12. You spirit of spiritual laziness, I bind you and cast you out of my life, you are no longer allowed in my life.

13. I refuse to be a victim in the race of life.
14. O God my Father, give me the grace to win the battles of life.
15. O God my Father, pour upon me the overcomer's anointing.
16. O God my Father, deliver me from my past failures and mistakes.
17. O God my Father, restore back onto me whatever I have lost by virtue of any delay in my life.
18. O God my Father, restore back onto me whatever I have lost by virtue of any delay in my marriage.
19. O God my Father, restore back onto me whatever I have lost by virtue of any delay in my church.
20. O God my Father, with you all things are possible, turn every failure and mistake in my life to a miracle.
21. O God my Father, with you all things are possible, turn every failure and mistake in my finances to a miracle.
22. O God my Father, with you all things are possible, turn every failure and mistake in my marriage to a miracle.
23. O God my Father, let all my potential that the enemy has destroyed be restored back to me.
24. O God my Father, take any "BUT" out of my life.
25. O God my Father, take any "BUT" out of my spiritual life.
26. O God my Father, take any "BUT" out of my destiny.
27. O God my Father, take any "BUT" out of my marriage.
28. I decree that nobody shall shine with my glory.
29. I decree that I shall not labor for others to eat.
30. I shall eat and enjoy the fruit of my labor.
31. O God my Father, give me a tangible reason to celebrate before the end of this prayer program.

32. O God my Father, stop my enemies as you stopped Pharaoh.

33. O God my Father, stop my enemies as you stopped Haman.

34. O God my Father, stop all my adversaries as you stopped Daniel's accusers in Babylon.

35. O God my Father, stop my household wickedness as you stopped Saul from destroying David.

36. O God my Father, let every Haman in my life begin to announce my glory.

37. O God my Father, let my Balaam bless me by force.

38. Lord, do what will make my enemies to know that you are my God.

39. Any power assigned to make me suffer, you will not escape the judgment of God.

40. O God my Father, no battle is forever, let my season of rest begin now.

41. O God my Father, give me grace to be courageous in every area of my life.

42. O God my Father, grant me the grace to become what you have destined me to be.

43. I receive the grace of God to recover all my stolen and buried potential.

44. O God my Father, increase my joy in every area, my joy will not turn to sorrow.

45. Every formless situation in my life, receive solution now.

46. Every void in any area of my life, receive solution now.

47. O God my Father, let your light disgrace every darkness in my life.

48. O God my Father, let your spirit bring transformation into every area of my life.

I WILL NOT GO DOWN

Passages To Read Before You Pray:
Isaiah 54:1-17, Ezekiel 37:1-11, Psalms 9, 86, 118

PRAYER POINTS

1. O God my Father, I thank you for your Word is yes and amen, and your Word will surely come to pass in my life.
2. O God my Father, I thank you for the good things that you have started in my life and you will perfect in the name of Jesus Christ.
3. O God my Father, I thank you for always being there for me and with me in the name of Jesus Christ.
4. O God my Father, when I find myself in the time of trouble, when all hope is lost, thank you for being there for me.
5. Father Lord, on the basis of your mercy, forgive me of all my sins and cleanse me in the blood of Jesus Christ.
6. I shall not go down, I will not be demoted.
7. O God my Father, withdraw the confidence and power source of my enemies.
8. O God my Father, withdraw the spiritual support of my enemies.
9. O God my Father, you are not a respecter of persons, do unto my enemies what you did to Haman.
10. I return to sender any form of barrenness manifesting in my life.
11. I return to sender any form of barrenness manifesting in my business.

12. I return to sender any form of barrenness manifesting in my marriage.
13. I return to sender any form of barrenness manifesting in my family.
14. I return to sender any form of barrenness manifesting in my spiritual life.
15. I return to sender any form of barrenness manifesting in my finances.
16. I return to sender any form of barrenness targeted at my destiny.
17. O God my Father, in the midst of the storm, hold my hand and never let me go.
18. I prophecy today that my future is full of miracles.
19. I prophecy today that there is celebration in my house.
20. I prophecy today that my harvest will be plenteous.
21. I hereby decree that great and mighty things begin to manifest in my life.
22. I prophecy today that doors of opportunities are opening unto me.
23. I prophecy today that I am moving from the bottom of the ladder to the top.
24. I prophecy today that my season of celebration begins now.
25. I prophecy today that heaven is releasing abundance into my life.
26. From this moment onward, lack will never be mentioned in my house ever again.
27. I declare today that my heavens of prosperity open now.
28. I declare today that my doors of blessing open now.
29. I will possess the gates of my enemies.
30. I move from the valley to the mountain top.
31. The glory of God is released upon my life.

32. The glory of God is released into my spiritual life.
33. No matter the situation around me, my life is moving forward.
34. I command every dead glory in my life to receive the life of God.
35. I prophecy, my season of testimony begins now.

DIVINE CONNECTION

Passages To Read Before You Pray:
1 Kings 17:8-16, Psalms 28, 40, 121, Isaiah 41:10-13, 50:7-10

PRAYER POINTS

1. O God my Father, I thank you for your Word is yes and amen, and your Word will surely come to pass in my life.
2. O God my Father, I thank you for the good things that you have started in my life and you will perfect in the name of Jesus Christ.
3. O God my Father, I thank you for always being there for me and with me in the name of Jesus Christ.
4. O God my Father, when I find myself in the time of trouble, when all hope is lost, thank you for being there for me.
5. Father Lord, on the basis of your mercy, forgive me of all my sins and cleanse me in the blood of Jesus Christ.
6. O God my Father, connect me to someone who has the solution to my situation in the name of Jesus Christ.
7. O God my Father, let my helpers have problems that only me can solve, in the name of Jesus Christ.
8. O God my Father, connect me to someone who has the key that will open the doors of my breakthroughs in the name of Jesus Christ.
9. O God my Father, connect me to someone who has the key that will open the door of my blessings in the name of Jesus Christ.

10. O God my Father, connect me to someone who has the key that will open the door of great opportunities for me in the name of Jesus Christ.
11. O God my Father, connect me to the people that you have prepared to contribute to my success in the name of Jesus Christ.
12. Today I command my helpers to step up and help me in the name of Jesus Christ.
13. O God my Father, connect me to someone who knows the way that will lead me to greatness in the name of Jesus Christ.
14. O God my Father, direct and help me to locate the people you have prepared to help me in the name of Jesus Christ.
15. O God my Father, no matter the situation around me, make divine provision to sustain me, in the name of Jesus Christ.
16. O God my Father, no matter how troublesome the storm of my life, make divine provision to rescue me in the name of Jesus Christ.
17. I will not miss the divine appointment with my helpers, in the name of Jesus Christ.
18. I will not miss the divine appointment with someone who has the solution to my situation in the name of Jesus Christ.
19. I will not miss the divine appointment to receive my miracles in the name of Jesus Christ.
20. I will not miss the divine appointment to receive my blessings in the name of Jesus Christ.
21. I will not miss the divine appointment to receive my breakthroughs in the name of Jesus Christ.
22. I will not miss my moment in the name of Jesus Christ.

23. O God my Father, let my helpers have problems that will lead them to connect with me in the name of Jesus Christ.
24. O God my Father, help me to recognize my helpers when I meet them, in the name of Jesus Christ.
25. O God my Father, connect me to the people that are willing and ready to go the extra miles to help me, in the name of Jesus Christ.
26. O God my Father, connect me to the people that will make helping me their top priority, in the name of Jesus Christ.
27. O God my Father, connect me to someone who has the last piece of the puzzle to my breakthroughs, in the name of Jesus Christ.
28. O God my Father, connect me to someone who has the last piece of the puzzle to my greatness, in the name of Jesus Christ.
29. O God my Father, connect me to someone who has the last piece of the puzzle to my financial freedom, in the name of Jesus Christ.
30. O God my Father, connect me to someone who has the last piece of the puzzle to the fulfillment of my dreams, in the name of Jesus Christ.
31. O God my Father, connect me to someone who has the last piece of the puzzle to my great achievement, in the name of Jesus Christ.
32. O God my Father, connect me to someone who has the answer to the greatest questions of my life, in the name of Jesus Christ.
33. O God my Father, connect me to me someone who is willing to show me how to make it in life, in the name of Jesus Christ.

34. O God my Father, connect me with good people in life in the name of Jesus Christ.
35. O God my Father, connect me to the people that will contribute to my spiritual growth, in the name of Jesus Christ.
36. O God my Father, connect me to the people that will love me more than their own life like Jonathan and David, in the name of Jesus Christ.
37. O God my Father, connect me to someone who will lead me to the top, in the name of Jesus Christ.
38. O God my Father, connect me to the people in the high places who will be willing to pull me up, in the name of Jesus Christ.
39. O God my Father, connect me to the kings and princes of this world, in the name of Jesus Christ.
40. O God my Father, connect me to the rich and wealthy, in the name of Jesus Christ.
41. My helpers will not disobey God, they will help me according to the plan of God in the name of Jesus Christ.
42. Connection that will make me become very great in life, begin to happen now in the name of Jesus Christ.
43. My helpers will not rest until they locate me and help me in the name of Jesus Christ.
44. That person who will help, wherever you are, I command you to come forth now in the name of Jesus Christ.
45. Connection that will change my situation for the better, I command it to happen now in the name of Jesus Christ.

DIVINE FAVOR FOR JOB INTERVIEW

Passages To Read Before You Pray:
Exodus 3:20-21, 11:3, 1 Samuel 16:22, Esther 2:15, Psalms 23, 42, 81, 121

PRAYER POINTS

1. O God my Father, I thank you for always being there for me and for always being there with me, in the name of Jesus Christ.
2. O God my Father, I thank you for this opportunity to go for a job interview, I know it is only you that can do this, blessed be your holy name.
3. Today O Lord, I repent of anything that I have done in the past or still doing against will, forgive me O Lord and cleanse me in the blood of Jesus Christ.
4. O God my Father, let your presence go before me today and grant me unusual favor in every area in the name of Jesus Christ.
5. Today O Lord, cover me with your glory, anyone that sees me will see you in me and all around me in the name of Jesus Christ.
6. I command every mountain of fear in my life to disappear in the name of Jesus Christ.
7. I command every mountain of doubt in my life to disappear in the name of Jesus Christ.
8. I command every mountain of unbelief in my life to disappear in the name of Jesus Christ.
9. I hereby command anxiety to depart from me and never come back again in the name of Jesus Christ.

10. I hereby cover myself in the precious blood of Jesus Christ.
11. I cover my resume and job application in the blood of Jesus Christ.
12. O God my Father, let the person that will interview me today see your glory upon my life, in the name of Jesus Christ.
13. O God my Father, let the person that will interview me see many reasons to give me the job, in the name of Jesus Christ.
14. As I open my mouth to speak at this interview, Father Lord, fill my mouth with words of wisdom, in the name of Jesus Christ.
15. As I open my mouth to speak at this interview, Father Lord, speak through me and let the interviewer hear your voice, in the name of Jesus Christ.
16. As I open my mouth to speak at this interview, Father Lord, fill my mouth with the word of knowledge that I may speak solution to this company's problems, in the name of Jesus Christ.
17. As I open my mouth to speak at this interview, Father Lord, fill my mouth with the word of knowledge that I may bring perfect ideas for the growth of the company, in the name of Jesus Christ.
18. O God my Father, let the employer see me as an asset they cannot afford to lose, in the name of Jesus Christ.
19. O God my Father, as I am going for this interview, cover me with your favor in the name of Jesus Christ.
20. O God my Father, let every decision made by the interviewer favor me, in the name of Jesus Christ.

21. O God my Father, let every decision made by the human resources director about this job interview favor me, in the name of Jesus Christ.

22. O God my Father, let the Holy Spirit convince the employer to hire me for this job opening, in the name of Jesus Christ.

23. I decree today that this job interview will be successful because the Lord is with me, in the name of Jesus Christ.

24. I will not make any mistake at this job interview in the name of Jesus Christ.

25. O God my Father, grant me your grace to speak the right word at the right time, in the name of Jesus Christ.

26. O God my Father, grant me your grace to have the right answer to every question at this job interview, in the name of Jesus Christ.

27. O God my Father, I want you to be the third person at this interview today, in the name of Jesus Christ.

28. O God my Father, I want you to be the chairman of this interview today, in the name of Jesus Christ.

29. O God my Father, I want you to be the moderator of this interview today, in the name of Jesus Christ.

30. O God my Father, let the person that will interview me go the extra miles to favor me at this job interview, in the name of Jesus Christ.

31. O God my Father, let those that will decide on whom to hire make an extra effort to hire me for this job opening, in the name of Jesus Christ.

32. O God my Father, let my name be placed above every other name at this job interview in the name of Jesus Christ.

33. O God my Father, let my name be favored above every other name for this job in the name of Jesus Christ.

34. O God my Father, by your grace and mercy, I claim this job today in the name of Jesus Christ.
35. I hereby decree that this job interview will be my last interview because I am getting this job, in the name of Jesus Christ.
36. O God my Father, let my job search come to a favorable end today, in the name of Jesus Christ.
37. O God my Father, let my job search come to a glorious end today in the name of Jesus Christ.
38. I will come back from this job interview rejoicing in the name of Jesus Christ.
39. I will come back from this job interview celebrating in the name of Jesus Christ.
40. I will come back from this job interview testifying to the goodness of God, in the name of Jesus Christ.

IT IS A NEW SEASON

Passages To Read Before You Pray:
Proverbs 23:18, Isaiah 43:1-21, Jeremiah 33:14, Psalm 126, Joel 2:19-27

PRAYER POINTS

1. O God my Father, I thank you for your faithfulness manifesting in my life day by day.
2. O God my Father, I thank you for being my great provider, providing for all my needs, spiritually, physically, financially and materially.
3. O God my Father, forgive me of all my sins and cleanse me from all unrighteousness.
4. I hereby cover myself and my household in the blood of Jesus Christ.
5. O God my Father, let struggle come to an end in my life today.
6. O God my Father, I refuse to fail, let the manifestation of failure in my life come to an end now.
7. O God my Father, I refuse to suffer, let the suffering in my life come to an end now.
8. O God my Father, I refuse to be poor, I reject poverty in every area of my life.
9. I command the spirit of poverty to depart from me now and never come back.
10. Any power anywhere, using me against myself to stop what God is doing in my life, you will not escape the judgment of God.

11. Any power anywhere, using me against myself to drive my helpers away from me you will not escape the judgment of God.
12. Any power anywhere, using me against myself to destroy my harvest, you will not escape the judgment of God.
13. You spirit of anger, you will not hinder my miracles this year, I bind and cast you out of my life.
14. You spirit of anger, you will not rob me of my blessings, I bind and cast you out of my life.
15. You spirit of anger, you cannot destroy what God is doing in my life, I bind and cast you out of my life.
16. You spirit of anger, you are not of God, loose your hold upon my life now.
17. O God my Father, let there be an end to the manifestation of anger in my life.
18. In this year, low self-esteem will not keep me at the bottom of the ladder.
19. O God my Father let the anointing and grace to be confident and bold in whatever I do rest upon me.
20. Any power anywhere, trying to kick me out of the race of life, you will not prosper, be disappointed.
21. O God my Father, lift me up and let me be above all my competitors in every area.
22. O God my Father, let the anointing for excellence rest upon me, I will excel in whatsoever I do.
23. In the midst of my colleagues and business partners, I will stand out.
24. In the midst of my family and friends, I will stand out.
25. I reject retrogression in every area of my life.
26. My life is moving forward.
27. I receive the grace of God to walk into my success.

28. I receive the grace of God to walk into my breakthrough.
29. O God my Father, bless me and make me a blessing to my generation.
30. O God my Father, let anyone that bless me be blessed, and whosoever curse me will be cursed.

IT IS HIGH TIME

Passages To Read Before You Pray:
Roman 13:11-14, Psalms 24, 29, 68, 80, 83, 86

PRAYER POINTS

1. O God my Father, I thank you for your Word is yes and amen, and your Word will surely come to pass in my life.
2. O God my Father, I thank you for the good things that you have started in my life and you will perfect in the name of Jesus Christ.
3. O God my Father, I thank you for always being there for me and with me in the name of Jesus Christ.
4. O God my Father, when I find myself in the time of trouble, when all hope is lost, thank you for being there for me.
5. Father Lord, on the basis of your mercy, forgive me of all my sins and cleanse me in the blood of Jesus Christ.
6. Anybody anywhere that is still holding my blessings, release my blessings to me now.
7. Anybody anywhere that has the power to help me but refuses to do so, I command you, arise and help me now.
8. This year is not over until I receive my blessings, wherever my blessings are, come forth and locate me.
9. This year is not over until I receive my breakthrough whenever my breakthrough is, come forth and locate me.

10. This year is not over until I receive my breakthrough whenever my breakthrough is, come forth and locate me now.
11. This year is not over until my heaven of abundance is open, O heaven of abundance, open unto me now.
12. This year is not over until my heaven of promotion is open, O heaven of promotion, open unto me now.
13. This year is not over until my heaven of answered prayers is open, O heaven of answered prayers, open unto me now.
14. This year is not over until my heaven of success is open, O heaven of success, open unto me now.
15. This year is not over until my heaven of financial freedom is open, O heaven of financial freedom, open now.
16. This year is not over until I get out of the pit of hopelessness, O God my father, send a rescue team now.
17. This year is not over until I receive solution to my situation, O God of possibility, let solution come now.
18. This year is not over until I have my testimonies, Father, let my testimonies come now without delay.
19. This year is not over until you fulfill your promises in my life, O God arise and fulfill your promise.
20. This year is not over until my life and situation is transformed, father lord, let the transformation begin.
21. O God my Father this is my moment, the moment I have been waiting for.

MY EXPECTATION SHALL NOT BE CUT OFF

Passages To Read Before You Pray:
1 king 8:56, Proverbs 23:18, 24:14, Jeremiah 33:14, Romans 4:21, 2 Corinthians 1:20

PRAYER POINTS

1. O God my Father, I thank you for being a wonderful and a good God in my life.
2. O God my Father, I thank you for always being with me even when I didn't know it.
3. O God my Father, reveal yourself unto me, I want to see you in your glory and majesty.
4. O God my Father, forgive me of all my sins and cleanse me from all unrighteousness.
5. I cover myself and my household in the blood of Jesus.
6. I will not pray in vain, my prayers will produce desired results.
7. I will not pray in vain, my prayers will bring forth testimonies.
8. I will not pray in vain, signs and wonders will follow my prayers.
9. I will not pray in vain, miracles will follow my prayer.
10. I will not pray in vain, my prayers will bring forth uncommon breakthroughs.
11. I will not pray in vain, my prayers will bring total deliverance into every area of my life.
12. I will not pray in vain, my prayers will bring perfect healing into every area of my life.

13. I will not pray in vain, my prayers shall provoke open heavens.
14. I will not pray in vain, my prayers shall provoke angelic assistance in every area of my life.
15. I will not pray in vain, my prayers shall provoke financial freedom in every area of my life.
16. I am expecting to succeed in everything I do; my expectation will not be cut off.
17. I am expecting to have success in my home and marriage; my expectation will not be cut off.
18. I am expecting to have success in my business and ministry; my expectation will not be cut off.
19. I am expecting my miracles to manifest before the end of this month; my expectation will not be cut off.
20. I am expecting my testimonies to come before the end of this month; my expectation will not be cut off.
21. I am expecting great and mighty things to happen in my life, my expectation will not be cut off.
22. I am expecting breakthroughs now in my business; my expectation will not be cut off.
23. I am expecting breakthroughs now in my ministry; my expectation will not be cut off.
24. I am expecting someone that will help me to get out of financial mess to locate me before the end of this month; my expectation will not be cut off.
25. I am expecting someone that will lead and guide me unto my promise land to locate me before the end of this month; my expectation will not be cut off.
26. I am expecting a positive turn around in every area of my life; my expectation will not be cut off.
27. I am expecting all my helpers to begin to locate me now; my expectation will not be cut off.

28. I am expecting this year to be the year of fulfillment of God's promises in my life; my expectation will not be cut off.
29. I am expecting the goodness and mercy of God to follow me every day of my life; my expectation will not be cut off.
30. I am expecting to be what God wants me to be and fulfill my God given purpose; my expectation will not be cut off.

PRAYER FOR YOUR BUSINESS

Passages To Read Before You Pray:
Leviticus 26:5, Deuteronomy 30:9, Psalms 1, 23, 132, Isaiah 30:23, Joel 2:19-24

PRAYER POINTS

1. God my Father, I thank you for the great privilege that you have given me to be called your child.
2. O God my Father, I thank you for always being there for me and with me in every area of my life.
3. Father Lord, I thank you for how far you have brought me and where you are taking me; for I know that you will take me to where you have designed for me to be.
4. O God my Father, forgive me of all my sin and mistakes, cleanse me from all unrighteousness and make me whole by the blood of Jesus Christ.
5. As I have come to you in prayer today O Lord, I refuse to pray in vain, my prayers will produce the desired results, in the name of Jesus Christ.
6. Today O Lord, breath the breath of life into my business and let my business come alive in every area, in the name of Jesus Christ.
7. Today O Lord, touch every area of my business with the power of resurrection in the name of Jesus Christ.
8. O God my Father, let my dying business be revived by your power and grace, in the name of Jesus Christ.
9. No matter the situation of the economy, my business will survive, in the name of Jesus Christ.

10. No matter the situation of the economy, my business will prosper, in the name of Jesus Christ.
11. No matter the situation of the economy my business will flourish in the name of Jesus Christ.
12. With all the authority and power in the name of Jesus Christ, I speak progress into every area of my business.
13. With all the authority and power in the name of Jesus Christ, I speak expansion into every area of my business.
14. With all the authority and power in the name of Jesus Christ, I speak growth into every area of my business.
15. O God my Father, dispatch your angels to advertise my business to the right people that need my service/products in the name of Jesus Christ.
16. O God my Father, empower my business to prosper in the name of Jesus Christ.
17. O God my Father, let there be a positive turn around in every area of my business in the name of Jesus Christ.
18. O God my Father, let the anointing for productivity rest upon my business now and forever, in the name of Jesus Christ.
19. O God my Father, let the season of harvest begin in every area of my business in the name of Jesus Christ.
20. O God my Father, let there be restoration in every area of my business in the name of Jesus Christ.
21. O God my Father, let there be open heavens upon my business from now and forever more in the name of Jesus Christ.
22. By the authority in the name of Jesus Christ, today I decree that my business will not fail no matter the activity of the enemies in the name of Jesus Christ.

23. O God my Father, let the people that will contribute to the success of my business locate me today in the name of Jesus Christ.
24. O God my Father, let the people that will help with good business ideas locate me now in the name of Jesus Christ.
25. O God my Father, give me money yielding ideas in the name of Jesus Christ.
26. Today I decree that I will experience breakthroughs in every area of my business now and forever in the name of Jesus Christ.
27. O God my Father, connect me to the right people that will help my business to move forward in the name of Jesus Christ.
28. O God my Father, open new doors of opportunity for me in the area of my business in the name of Jesus Christ.
29. O God my Father, let new things begin happen in my business in the name of Jesus Christ.
30. O God my Father, let good and beautiful things begin to happen and manifest in my business so that people may know that I serve a good God, in the name of Jesus Christ.

RE-ARRANGE MY LIFE O LORD

Passages To Read Before You Pray:
Joel 2:21, Habakkuk 1:5, Jeremiah 33:3, Psalms 23, 29, 59, 69

PRAYER POINTS

1. O God my Father, I thank you for your Word is yes and amen, and your Word will surely come to pass in my life.
2. O God my Father, I thank you for the good things that you have started in my life and you will perfect it in the name of Jesus Christ.
3. O God my Father, I thank you for always being there for me and with me in the name of Jesus Christ.
4. O God my Father, when I find myself in the time of trouble, when all hope is lost, thank you for being there for me.
5. Father Lord, on the basis of your mercy, forgive me of all my sins and cleanse me in the blood of Jesus Christ.
6. O God my Father, separate me from the misfortune that has been following me from the beginning of this year in the name of Jesus Christ.
7. I will not end this year in regret in the name of Jesus Christ.
8. I will not end up as a failure in the name of Jesus Christ.
9. I will not end this year in disappointment in the name of Jesus Christ.
10. O God my Father, use this prayer program to transform my life to your original plan for me in the name of Jesus Christ.

11. O God my Father, use this prayer program to bring the fulfillment of your promises for my life in the name of Jesus Christ.
12. O God my Father, in this prayer program, perform your miracles in my life in the name of Jesus Christ.
13. In this prayer program O Lord, rescue me from the pit of hopelessness in the name of Jesus Christ.
14. O God my Father, re-arrange my life for breakthroughs today in the name of Jesus Christ.
15. O God my Father, re-arrange my life for prosperity today in the name of Jesus Christ.
16. O God my Father, re-arrange my life for success today in the name of Jesus Christ.
17. Every cycle of frustration in any area of my life, break now in the name of Jesus Christ.
18. Every cycle of failure in any area of my life, break in the name of Jesus Christ.
19. Every cycle of disappointment in any area of my life, break in the name of Jesus Christ.
20. Every cycle of rejection in any area of my life, break in the name of Jesus Christ.
21. No matter the situation around me, my life is moving forward from glory to glory in the name of Jesus Christ.
22. O God my Father, do something unusually good in my life today, that will make the whole world read and listen to my testimony in the name of Jesus Christ.
23. Any power that has been delaying my blessings since the beginning of this year, receive sudden destruction in the name of Jesus Christ.
24. I shall not drown in the rivers of life in the name of Jesus Christ.

25. I shall not drown over my past mistakes in the name of Jesus Christ.
26. I shall not drown over my past defeat in the name of Jesus Christ.
27. I shall not drown over my past failures in the name of Jesus Christ.
28. I shall not drown over my past delays in the name of Jesus Christ.
29. I shall not drown over my past betrayals in the name of Jesus Christ.
30. No matter the situation around me, before the end of this prayer program I will sing a new song, in the name of Jesus Christ.
31. No matter the situation around me, before the end of this prayer program I will dance a new dance in the name of Jesus Christ.
32. No matter the situation around me, before the end of this prayer program I will have reasons to testify in the name of Jesus Christ.
33. Any power that is prolonging affliction in my life, you will not escape the judgment of God in the name of Jesus Christ.
34. Any power that is prolonging my financial problems, you will not escape the judgment of God in the name of Jesus Christ.
35. Any power that is prolonging unpleasant situations in my life, you will not escape the judgment of God in the name of Jesus Christ.
36. Any power that is prolonging my problems, you will not escape the judgment of God in the name of Jesus Christ.
37. The Lord has crowned me with glory and honor, I will not end my life in shame in the name of Jesus Christ.

38. O God my Father, arise and use me to re-write the story of my family in the name of Jesus Christ.
39. You spirit of planning and not executing, I bind you and cast you out of my life in the name of Jesus Christ.
40. Evil pattern of rising and falling in my life, be destroyed by the fire of God, in the name of Jesus Christ.
41. Evil pattern of rising and falling in my business, be destroyed by the fire of God in the name of Jesus Christ.
42. Evil pattern of rising and falling in my finances, be destroyed by the fire of God in the name of Jesus Christ.
43. Because Jesus is my Lord, my life shall be better now than ever before in the name of Jesus Christ.
44. Because Jesus is my Lord, my business shall be better now than ever before in the name of Jesus Christ.
45. Because Jesus died for me, my relationship with God shall be better now than ever before in the name of Jesus Christ.

TOTAL DELIVERANCE

Passages To Read Before You Pray:
Matthew 8:28-24, 9:32-38, Luke 9:1, Mark 16:17-18, Psalms 18, 35, 59, 70, 109

PRAYER POINTS

1. O God my Father, I thank you for what you are doing in my life.
2. O God my Father, I thank you for the great privilege to be called your child.
3. O God my Father, I thank you for fighting my battles and giving me the victory.
4. O God my Father, forgive me of all my sins and cleanse me in the blood of Jesus.
5. Today O Lord, I want to see you like never before, open the eyes of my heart.
6. I cover myself and my household in the blood of Jesus Christ.
7. With the authority and power in the name of Jesus, I command every spirit assigned to torment me to get out of my life and never come back.
8. With the authority and power in the name of Jesus, I command every spirit assigned to make my life miserable to get out of my life and come back no more.
9. With the authority and power in the name of Jesus, I command any spirit assigned to hold me back from fulfilling purpose to get out of my life and come back no more.

10. With the authority and power in the name of Jesus, I claim total deliverance today from any form of bondage.

11. With the authority and power in the name of Jesus, I command every plan of the enemy against me this year to be disappointed and fail.

12. With the authority and power in the name of Jesus, I am getting out of the pit of hopelessness.

13. With the authority and power in the name of Jesus, I command all the works, of the devil manifesting in my life to be destroyed.

14. With the authority and power in the name of Jesus, I am getting out of my Egypt today.

15. With the authority and power in the name of Jesus, I command Red Sea to give way for me to cross over.

16. I will not die in Egypt in the name of Jesus Christ.

17. I receive the grace and power of God to overcome any situation in my life.

18. I receive the power and the grace of God to overcome any problem manifesting in my life.

19. I refuse to be a victim of demonic attack.

20. I command every bondage in my life to break into irreparable prices.

21. I command every chain that keeps me in bondage to be destroyed by fire.

22. I command every evil mark upon my life to be erased by the blood of Jesus.

23. O God my Father, arise and fight for me.

24. O God my Father, arise and prove to the enemies that you are my God.

25. O God my Father, arise and set me free from every situation in my life.

26. In your presence O Lord my case will not be impossible.

27. O God my Father, let there be divine intervention in every area of my life now.
28. Any door in my life that I have ignorantly opened to the enemy, father, let it be permanently closed forever.
29. Today O Lord, have mercy and rescue me.
30. Today O Lord, let there be a total and complete deliverance in every area of my life.

REMOVING THE GATES OF BRASS

Passages To Read Before You Pray:
Genesis 28:13, Psalms 46, 83, 86, 106, Isaiah 43:1-7, 45:1-3,
Jeremiah 33:14

PRAYER POINTS

1. O God my Father, I thank you for the privilege you have given me to be called your child.
2. O God my Father, I thank you for your grace and mercy that I enjoy day after day.
3. I confess my sins before you today O Lord, forgive me and cleanse me in the blood of Jesus Christ.
4. According to the book of Genesis 28:13, O God my Father, reveal yourself unto me in a marvelous way today.
5. I cover myself in the precious blood of Jesus Christ.
6. O God my Father, uphold me with your right hand of righteousness with the journey of this year, I don't want to walk alone in Jesus name.
7. O God my Father, let the Holy Spirit guide me in every step I will take this year.
8. O God my Father, let the Holy Spirit guide me in every decision I will make this year in Jesus name.
9. Every seed of greatness in me, be fertilized by the Holy Ghost and begin to manifest in Jesus name.
10. Seed of greatness in me, receive a touch from God and manifest now.

11. Every cloud of unbelief that is covering my greatness, this is my year, I command you to disappear in Jesus name.
12. Every work of the devil assigned to hinder my greatness, this is my year, I command you to be destroyed. – 1 John 3:8.
13. Spirit of almost there assigned to rob me of my greatness, this is my year; you will not prosper in Jesus name.
14. It is my turn, O God my Father, let my greatness manifest without any hindrance or delay in Jesus name.
15. O God my Father, let the anointing for multiplication rest upon me.
16. O God my Father, let the anointing for multiplication rest upon the works of my hands.
17. O God my Father, let the anointing for multiplication rest upon my finances.
18. Today O Lord, bless me and my household with the blessings of heaven.
19. No matter the situation around me, I will be exceedingly fruitful in the name of Jesus Christ.
20. O God my Father, let the anointing for multiplication rest upon the seeds of my field in Jesus name.
21. Anointing to possess and eat the good of this land, rest upon me now, in the name of Jesus Christ.
22. O God my Father, let my greatness be revealed to the world this year, in the name of Jesus Christ.
23. Any power anywhere fighting against my greatness, you will not escape the judgment of God.
24. Today, I receive the grace of God to possess the gates of my enemies, in the name of Jesus Christ.

25. I will spread to the south, to the north, to the east, and to the west, in the name of Jesus Christ

26. If no one can hinder the sun from rising, no power will be able to hinder my greatness from manifesting in Jesus name.

27. No matter the efforts and activities of the enemy, I will be great on earth in Jesus name.

28. O God my Father, go before me into the remaining days and months of this year, and remove every stubborn mountain out of my way in Jesus name.

29. It is my turn to fulfill destiny, you mountain of impossibilities, I command you to disappear.

30. I refuse to suffer in life, Father, make it easy for me to breakthrough, in the name of Jesus Christ.

31. I refuse to struggle in life, Father, let the anointing of ease rest upon me now in Jesus name.

32. I refuse to labor in vain, I will eat the fruit of my labor.

33. I refuse to work for another to eat, in the name of Jesus Christ.

34. O God my Father, let every crooked place in my life be made straight today, in the name of Jesus Christ.

35. In my life today O Lord, let every mountain be brought low and every valley to be exalted.

36. O God my Father, let your glory be revealed in my life for the whole world to see.

37. Every day of my life, the Lord is with me, I will not be afraid.

38. Every gate of brass standing between me and my breakthrough, be broken into irreparable pieces in the name of Jesus Christ.

39. Every gate of brass standing between me and my helpers be broken into irreparable pieces.

40. Every gate of brass blocking my access into the promise land, be broken into irreparable pieces.
41. Every gate of brass designed to block my miracles this year, be broken into irreparable pieces.
42. Every gate of brass designed to keep me away from my open heavens, be broken into irreparable pieces.
43. Every gate of brass designed to keep me away from the source of my joy be broken into irreparable pieces.
44. Every gate of brass designed to stop my progress be broken into irreparable pieces.
45. Every gate of brass designed to delay my financial freedom be broken into irreparable pieces.
46. Every gate of brass designed to stop me from getting to the top, be broken into irreparable pieces.
47. Every gate of brass designed to stop the riches and wealth from flowing into my life, be broken into irreparable pieces.
48. By the fire of the Holy Spirit, I receive access to the sources of my breakthroughs.
49. By the fire of the Holy Spirit, I claim back my stolen blessings in Jesus name.
50. Release your fire O Lord, and destroy every gate of brass built against me.

THE COUNSEL OF AHITOPHEL

Passages To Read Before You Pray:
1Chronicles 27:33, 2 Samuel 15:12, 31, 16:20-21, 17:1-3,
Psalms 35, 55, 83

- Ahitophel was the king's counselor
- He knows the in and out of the king's life
- He knows the king's strengths and weaknesses
- He knows when the king's is mostly vulnerable
- He knows every move and step of the king
- He knows the thoughts and decisions of the king
- He knows what to do to weaken the king.

PRAYER POINTS

1. O God my Father, I bless your name today for being a wonderful and a good God in every area of my life.
2. O God my Father, I thank you for always being there for me and with me, in the name of Jesus Christ.
3. O God my Father, I thank you for answering my prayers day after day, time after time, in the name of Jesus Christ.
4. On the basis of your mercy O Lord, forgive me of my sins and cleanse me in the blood of Jesus Christ.
5. Today O Lord, answer my prayers once again by fire and let the world know that I serve a good God, in the name of Jesus Christ.
6. Today I refuse to pray in vain, my prayers must hit the target and produce the desired results, in the name of Jesus Christ.

7. O God my Father, let every Ahitophel in my camp be exposed and be disgraced, in the name of Jesus Christ.

8. O God my Father, let every Ahitophel among my friends be exposed and be disgraced, in the name of Jesus Christ.

9. O God my Father, let every Ahitophel in my father's house be exposed and be disgraced, in the name of Jesus Christ.

10. O God my Father, let every Ahitophel in my place of work be exposed and be disgraced, in the name of Jesus Christ.

11. O God my Father, let every Ahitophel in my neighborhood be exposed and be disgraced, in the name of Jesus Christ.

12. O God my Father, let the Ahitophel among my counselors be exposed and be disgraced, in the name of Jesus Christ.

13. O God my Father, let every unfriendly friend around me be exposed and be disgraced, in the name of Jesus Christ.

14. Any living soul that knows the in and out of my life, and is now working against me, you will not escape the judgment of God, in the name of Jesus Christ.

15. Any living soul that knows the in and out of my life, and is now working against my finances, you will not escape the judgment of God, in the name of Jesus Christ.

16. Any living soul that knows the in and out of my life, and is now working against my marriage, you will not escape the judgment of God, in the name of Jesus Christ.

17. Any living soul that knows the in and out of my life, and is now working against my joy, you will not escape the judgment of God, in the n are of Jesus Christ.

18. O God my Father, let the Ahitophel that joins forces with my enemies be disgraced, in the name of Jesus Christ.

19. O God my Father, turn the counsel of Ahitophel to foolishness in every area of my life, in the name of Jesus Christ.

20. The counsel of Ahitophel will not prevail against me in the name of Jesus Christ.

21. The counsel of Ahitophel will not prevail against my family in the name of Jesus Christ.

22. The counsel of Ahitophel will not prevail against my marriage in the name of Jesus Christ.

23. The counsel of Ahitophel will not prevail against my children in the name of Jesus Christ.

24. The counsel of Ahitophel will not prevail against my finances in the name of Jesus Christ.

25. The counsel of Ahitophel will not prevail against my destiny in the name of Jesus Christ.

26. The counsel of Ahitophel will not prevail against my business and career in the name of Jesus Christ.

27. The counsel of Ahitophel will not prevail against my future in the name of Jesus Christ.

28. Every activity of Ahitophel to weaken me will not prosper in the name of Jesus Christ.

29. Every plan of Ahitophel to attack me when I am vulnerable will not prosper in the name of Jesus Christ.

30. Every plan of Ahitophel to use my weakness against me will not prosper in the name of Jesus Christ.

31. I decree confusion into the camp of the Ahitophels of my life in the name of Jesus Christ.

32. O God my Father, let the Ahitophel of my life be disgraced and commit suicide in the name of Jesus Christ.
33. O God my Father, let the counsel of Ahitophel against me be used against him in the name of Jesus Christ.
34. O God my Father, raise my Husai that will counter the agenda of Ahitophel concerning my life, in the name of Jesus Christ.
35. O God my Father, raise my Husai that will confuse the plan of Ahitophel against my life in the name of Jesus Christ.

THE FIRE OF GOD

Passages To Read Before You Pray:
Exodus 3:2, 14:23-24, 18:19, 24:16-17, Leviticus 10:1-2, Ezekiel 1:4, Hebrews 12:29

PRAYER POINTS

1. O God my Father, I thank you for your Word is yes and amen, and your Word will surely come to pass in my life.
2. O God my Father, I thank you for the good things that you have started in my life and you will perfect it in the name of Jesus Christ.
3. O God my Father, I thank you for always being there for me and with me in the name of Jesus Christ.
4. O God my Father, when I find myself in the time of trouble, when all hope is lost, thank you for being there for me.
5. Father Lord, on the basis of your mercy, forgive me of all my sins and cleanse me in the blood of Jesus Christ.
6. O God my Father, reveal yourself unto me by your fire.
7. O God my Father, let your glory and majesty descend upon me today by fire and make my life untouchable to the enemy.
8. O God my Father, cover me with your glory and let any stranger power that comes near me be devoured by your fire.
9. O God my Father, cover me with your glory and when poverty comes near me, let it be devoured by your fire.

10. O God my Father, cover me with your glory and let all my problems be destroyed by your fire in the name of Jesus Christ.
11. O God my Father, cover me with your glory and all curses upon my life be devoured by your fire in the name of Jesus Christ.
12. O God my Father, cover me with your glory and let every strange hand upon my finances be destroyed by your fire in the name of Jesus Christ.
13. O God my Father, cover me with your glory and let every obstacles in my ways be destroyed by your fire in the name of Jesus Christ.
14. O God my Father, cover me with your glory and let the mark of failure upon my life be removed by your fire in the name of Jesus Christ.
15. O God my Father, cover me with your glory and let the expectation of the enemy in my life be disappointed in the name of Jesus Christ.
16. O God my Father, let you whirlwind scatter the camp of my enemies and let your fire destroy their evil plans against me in the name of Jesus Christ.
17. Every strange fire manifesting on my prayer altar, be quenched by the fire of God in the name of Jesus Christ.
18. Every strange fire working against my life, be quenched by the fire of God in the name of Jesus Christ.
19. Every strange fire working against my marriage, be quenched by the fire of God in the name of Jesus Christ.
20. Every strange fire working against my finances, be quenched by the fire of God in the name of Jesus Christ.
21. Every strange fire working against my joy, be quenched by the fire of God in the name of Jesus Christ.

22. Every strange fire creating confusion in my spiritual life, be quenched by the fire of God in the name of Jesus Christ.

23. O God my Father, let your presence with me trouble all the enemies around me by your fire in the name of Jesus Christ.

24. O God my Father, let your presence with me trouble my household wickedness by fire in the name of Jesus Christ.

25. O God my Father, let your presence with me trouble anyone spreading evil report about me in the name of Jesus Christ.

26. O God my Father, let your presence with me trouble my unrepentant enemies by your fire in the name of Jesus Christ.

27. O God my Father, let your presence with me trouble those that trouble me by your fire in the name of Jesus Christ.

28. O God my Father, let your presence with me trouble any power that is delaying my miracles in the name of Jesus Christ.

29. O God my Father, let your presence with me trouble any power blocking my breakthroughs in the name of Jesus Christ.

30. O God my Father, let your presence with me trouble any power that is hindering my success in the name of Jesus Christ.

31. O God my Father, let your presence with me trouble any power that is delaying my testimonies in the name of Jesus Christ.

32. O God my Father, let your presence with me trouble the Goliath of my father's house in the name of Jesus Christ.

33. O God my Father, let your presence with me trouble any power that wants me to labor in vain in the name of Jesus Christ.

34. O God my Father, let your presence with me trouble every Pharaoh of my father's house in the name of Jesus Christ.

35. O God my Father, let your presence with me bring fear upon the camp of my enemies in the name of Jesus Christ.

36. O God my Father, let your fire guide me day and night in every day of my life in the name of Jesus Christ.

37. As I lift up my voice in prayer, Father Lord, let your fire be released to destroy every agenda of the enemy against me in the name of Jesus Christ.

38. As I lift up my voice in prayer, Father Lord, let your fire be released to destroy every mountain of impossibility that is confronting me in the name of Jesus Christ.

39. As I lift up my voice in prayer, Father Lord, let your fire be released and let the seed of failure in my life be completely destroyed in the name of Jesus Christ.

40. As I lift up my voice in prayer, Father Lord, let your fire be released and let every mountain of disappointment be destroyed in the name of Jesus Christ.

41. As I lift up my voice in prayer, Father Lord, let your fire be released and let every seed of sickness in my life be completely destroyed in the name of Jesus Christ.

42. As I lift up my voice in prayer, Father Lord, let your fire be released and let every mark of poverty upon my life be completely removed in the name of Jesus Christ.

43. As I lift up my voice in prayer, Father Lord, let your fire be released and let stagnancy in my life be destroyed in the name of Jesus Christ.

44. As I lift up my voice in prayer, Father Lord, let your fire be released and let every evil covering upon my glory be removed in the name of Jesus Christ.

45. As I lift up my voice in prayer, Father Lord, let your fire be released and let any power that is attacking my finances be destroyed in the name of Jesus Christ.

46. As I lift up voice in prayer, Father Lord, let your fire be released and let any power that is attacking my marriage be destroyed in the name of Jesus Christ.

47. O God my Father, let your glory and majesty descend upon me and let my life be purified by your fire in the name of Jesus Christ.

48. O God my Father, let your glory and majesty descend upon me and let your fire re-arrange my life for miracles in the name of Jesus Christ.

49. O God my Father, let your glory and majesty descend upon me and let your fire re-arrange my life for breakthroughs in the name of Jesus Christ.

50. O God my Father, let your glory and majesty descend upon me and let your fire re-arrange my life for promotion in the name of Jesus Christ.

51. O God my Father, let your glory and majesty descend upon me and let your fire catapult me into greatness in the name of Jesus Christ.

52. O God my Father, let your glory and majesty descend upon me and let the time of my revelation come now in the name of Jesus Christ.

53. O God my Father, let your glory and majesty upon my life attract my helpers to help me in every area in the name of Jesus Christ.

54. O God my Father, let your glory and majesty upon my life attract people that will help me to get to the top in the name of Jesus Christ.
55. O God my Father, let your glory and majesty descend upon me and let your fire prepare me for the fulfillment of my purpose in the name of Jesus Christ.

BREAKING SATANIC CHAINS

Passages To Read Before You Pray:
John 11:43-44, Acts 12:1-17, 16:19-32, Psalms 46, 59, 69, 70

PRAYER POINTS

1. O God my Father, I thank you for your Word is yes and amen, and your Word will surely come to pass in my life.
2. O God my Father, I thank you for the good things that you have started in my life and you will perfect it in the name of Jesus Christ.
3. O God my Father, I thank you for always being there for me and with me in the name of Jesus Christ.
4. O God my Father, when I find myself in the time of trouble, when all hope is lost, thank you for being there for me.
5. I cover myself in the precious blood of Jesus Christ.
6. Have mercy upon me O Lord and forgive me of all my sins, cleanse me in the blood of Jesus Christ.
7. I baptize myself in the fire of the Holy Ghost.
8. Every satanic chain holding me down, break now in the name of Jesus Christ.
9. Every satanic chain holding my miracles, break now in the name of Jesus Christ.
10. Every satanic chain holding my progress, break now in the name of Jesus Christ.
11. Every satanic chain that will not let me move forward, be destroyed by the fire of God in the name of Jesus Christ.

12. Every satanic chain designed to keep me in the bondage of sickness, be destroyed by the fire of God in the name of Jesus Christ.
13. Every satanic chain prepared to keep me in the bondage of poverty, be destroyed by the fire of God in the name of Jesus Christ.
14. Every satanic chain prepared for me by household wickedness, be destroyed by the fire of God in the name of Jesus Christ.
15. Every satanic chain designed to make my life stagnant, be destroyed by the fire of God in the name of Jesus Christ.
16. Every invisible chain working against my destiny, be destroyed by the fire of God in the name of Jesus Christ.
17. Every satanic chain working against my success, be broken into irreparable pieces in the name of Jesus Christ.

THE BLOOD OF JESUS CHRIST

Passages To Read Before You Pray:
Exodus 12:12-13, 21-23, Hebrew 9:14, 12:24, Romans 5:9,
Revelation 1:5, 12:11, Numbers 22:29.

PRAYER POINTS

1. O God my Father, I thank you for your Word is yes and amen, and your Word will surely come to pass in my life.
2. O God my Father, I thank you for the good things that you have started in my life and you will perfect it in the name of Jesus Christ.
3. O God my Father, I thank you for always being there for me and with me in the name of Jesus Christ.
4. O God my Father, when I find myself in the time of trouble, when all hope is lost, thank you for being there for me.
5. Father Lord, on the basis of your mercy, forgive me of all my sins and cleanse me in the blood of Jesus Christ.
6. O God my Father, let the blood of Jesus plead my case against any accusing voice assigned against me.
7. O God my Father, let the blood of Jesus plead my case against any accusing voice speaking evil against my life.
8. O God my Father, let the blood of Jesus plead my case against any false prophet prophesying against me.
9. O God my Father, let the blood of Jesus plead my case against every Balaam hired to curse me.

10. No matter the situation around me, I will overcome by the blood of Jesus.
11. I apply the blood of Jesus against every unpleasant situation in my life and I command solution to come.
12. I apply the blood of Jesus against every mouth that is saying No to the Yes of God in my life.
13. O God my Father, let the blood of Jesus speak better things into my life.
14. O God my Father, let the blood of Jesus speak better things into my family.
15. O God my Father, let the blood of Jesus speak solution into my situation.
16. O God my Father, let the blood of Jesus speak peace and calmness to the storm of my life.
17. O God my Father, let the blood of Jesus speak better things into the life of my children.
18. O God my Father, let every evil mark upon my life be removed by the blood of Jesus Christ.
19. O God my Father, let every poverty identification mark upon my life be removed by the blood of Jesus.
20. O God my Father, let every mark of hatred upon my life be removed by the blood of Jesus Christ.
21. Every evil mark that is stopping people from helping me, be removed today by the blood of Jesus Christ.
22. Every evil mark that is driving my helpers away from me, be removed today by the blood of Jesus Christ.
23. Every evil mark that is causing my life to be stagnant be removed by the blood of Jesus Christ.
24. Every evil mark that is attracting problems to my life, be removed by the blood of Jesus Christ.
25. Every evil mark that is attracting the devourer to my finances, be removed by the blood of Jesus Christ.

26. Every evil mark that is causing my good efforts to be wasted, be removed by the blood of Jesus Christ.
27. Every evil mark that is causing me to pray without results, be removed by the blood of Jesus Christ.
28. Every evil mark that is causing me to wander away from my Goshen, be removed by the blood of Jesus Christ.
29. Every evil mark that will make me to leave my Bethlehem, the house of bread, be removed by the blood of Jesus.
30. Every evil mark that can make me to leave Canaan for Egypt, be removed by the blood of Jesus Christ.
31. By the blood of Jesus Christ, I overcome every challenge that may come my way.
32. By the blood of Jesus Christ, I overcome every activity of the enemy against my life.
33. By the blood of Jesus Christ, I overcome every attack of the enemy against my finances.
34. By the blood of Jesus Christ, I overcome every task master assigned to enslave me.
35. By the blood of Jesus Christ, I overcome every power assigned to delay my blessings.
36. By the blood of Jesus Christ, I overcome every power assigned to hinder my prayers.
37. By the blood of Jesus Christ, I overcome every power that is creating the atmosphere of confusion in my life.
38. By the blood of Jesus Christ, I overcome every power that is creating the atmosphere of confusion in my home.
39. By the blood of Jesus Christ, I overcome every power fighting against my destiny.
40. By the blood of Jesus Christ, I overcome every power fighting against the will of God in my life.

41. By the blood of Jesus Christ, I overcome sickness and sorrow.
42. By the blood of Jesus Christ, I overcome every disappointment in any area of my life.
43. By the blood of Jesus Christ, I overcome failure and rejection, in the name of Jesus Christ.

LET ME KNOW YOUR PLAN

Passages To Read Before You Pray:
Jeremiah 29:10-14, 33:14, Psalm 40, 42, 89, Isaiah 60:1-22,
61:1-11

PRAYER POINTS

1. O God my Father, I thank you for the wonderful plans that you have for me and my future, in the name of Jesus Christ.
2. O God my Father, I thank you for always being there for me and my household, in the name of Jesus Christ.
3. O God my Father, I thank you for grace and mercy that you extend to me day after day, time after time, in the name of Jesus Christ.
4. O God my Father, I thank you for being so faithful to me in every area of my life, I will forever praise your name, in the name of Jesus Christ.
5. On the basis of your mercy O Lord, forgive me of my sins and errors, and cleanse me in the blood of Jesus Christ.
6. I will not pray in vain, my prayer will produce the desired results in the name of Jesus Christ.
7. I cover myself and my family in the precious blood of Jesus Christ.
8. O God my Father, show me your plan for my life so that I may work in agreement with it and not against it, in the name of Jesus Christ.

9. O God my Father, let me know your plans for my spouse so that we may work in agreement with it and not against it, in the name of Jesus Christ.
10. O God my Father, let me know your plans for children so that we may work in agreement with it and not against it, in the name of Jesus Christ.
11. O God my Father, let me know your plans concerning my future, so that I may work in agreement with it and not against it, in the name of Jesus Christ.
12. O God my Father, let me know your plans concerning my business or career, so that I will not waste my time and efforts, in the name of Jesus Christ.
13. O God my Father, let me know your plans concerning every decision I will make in life, so that I will not do anything against your will, in the name of Jesus Christ.
14. Today O Lord, I submit my will to your will; let your will alone be done in every area of my life, in the name of Jesus Christ.
15. O God my Father, show me the next step I need to take in life so that I will not work against your plans for my life, in the name of Jesus Christ.
16. O God my Father, let your plans for my life prevail against the plans of the enemy, in the name of Jesus Christ.
17. I know your thoughts toward me are of peace and not of evil, let it come to physical manifestation in the name of Jesus Christ.
18. O God my Father, I know you plan to take me to a higher ground; sin will not hinder your plans for me, in the name of Jesus Christ.

19. O God my Father, I know you plan to bless me beyond expectation; works of the flesh will not hinder your plans for me, in the name of Jesus Christ.
20. O God my Father, I know you plan to take me to a higher level of grace; ignorance will not hinder your plans for me, in the name of Jesus Christ.
21. O God my Father, I know you plan to promote me according to your Word; pride will not hinder your plans for me, in the name of Jesus Christ.
22. O God my Father, show me what you want me to do in life in the name of Jesus Christ.
23. O God my Father, show me where you want me to be in life in the name of Jesus Christ.
24. O God my Father, grant me the grace to consult you before I make any plans in life, in the name of Jesus Christ.
25. I hereby cancel any plan of the wicked against my life, in the name of Jesus Christ.
26. I cancel every plan of the household wickedness against my marriage, in the name of Jesus Christ.
27. I cancel every plan of the enemy against my children, in the name of Jesus Christ.
28. I cancel every plan of the enemy against my destiny, in the name of Jesus Christ.
29. I cancel every plan of the wicked against my future, in the name of Jesus Christ.
30. I cancel every plan of the wicked against my finances, in the name of Jesus Christ.
31. Every plan of the enemy to pollute my joy, be terminated in the name of Jesus Christ.
32. Every plan of the enemy to hinder my progress, be terminated in the name of Jesus Christ.

33. Every plan of the enemy to delay my miracles, be terminated in the name of Jesus Christ.

34. I will not work against the plan of God for my life no matter the distraction, in the name of Jesus Christ.

35. I will not work against the plan of God for my life no matter the effort of the enemy, in the name of Jesus Christ.

36. O God my Father, let your plans for my life be crystal clear to me, that I will have no reason to doubt it, in the name of Jesus Christ.

37. O God my Father, let your plans for my life be crystal clear to me, that I may follow it as a road map, in the name of Jesus Christ.

38. O God my Father, let your will alone be done in every area of my life, in the name of Jesus Christ.

39. My plan will not hinder the plan of God for my life, in the name of Jesus Christ.

40. O God my Father, help me to see beyond the natural, so that I may follow your plan for my life, in the name of Jesus Christ.

41. O God my Father, help me to see beyond the ordinary, so that I may see where you are taking me, in the name of Jesus Christ.

42. O God my Father, help me to see beyond my present situation, so that I may see your glory in the name of Jesus Christ.

43. O God my Father, help me to see beyond the frustration that the enemy send my way, in the name of Jesus Christ.

44. O God my Father, help me to see beyond the agenda of the wicked, so that I may see your grace and mercy, in the name of Jesus Christ.

45. No matter the activity of the enemy, I will not fall out of the plan of God, in the name of Jesus Christ.
46. O God my Father, let your will power bring to manifestation all your plans for my life, in the name of Jesus Christ.
47. O God my Father, let your will power bring to manifestation all your plans concerning my future in the name of Jesus Christ.
48. O God my Father, let your will power bring to manifestation all your plans concerning my finances in the name of Jesus Christ.
49. O God my Father, let your will power bring to manifestation all your plans concerning my business or career in the name of Jesus Christ.
50. Today I decree that testimonies, miracles, signs and wonders will follow my prayers, in the name of Jesus Christ.

NO MORE FAILURE

Passages To Read Before You Pray:
2 Kings 3:17, Isaiah 41:15, 54:4, Esther 4:10-16, 8:16-17,
Psalms 30, 34, 56

PRAYER POINTS

1. O God my Father, I thank you for your Word is yes and amen, and your Word will surely come to pass in my life.
2. O God my Father, I thank you for the good things that you have started in my life and you will perfect it in the name of Jesus Christ.
3. O God my Father, I thank you for always being there for me and with me in the name of Jesus Christ.
4. O God my Father, when I find myself in the time of trouble, when all hope is lost, thank you for being there for me.
5. Father Lord, on the basis of your mercy, forgive me of all my sins and cleanse me in the blood of Jesus Christ.
6. O God my Father, let the power to receive answered prayers fall upon me now.
7. All hindrances get out of my way now in the name of Jesus Christ.
8. Stumbling blocks, get out of my way now in the name of Jesus Christ.
9. O God my Father, let this prayer be a life-changing encounter for me.
10. I decree today that there is no more shame for me.

11. I decree today that there is no more disgrace for me and my household.
12. I command every seed of shame in my life to be removed and destroyed.
13. Any power generating problems in my life, you will not escape the judgment of God.
14. By the power of Jesus, any mountain that is delaying my miracles, explode and scatter by the fire of God.
15. Wherever my name is mentioned for evil, let the fire of God answer them.
16. O God my Father, I command, that the king that will not favor me will lose his seat.
17. As from today, any shrine where my name is being mentioned, be destroyed by the fire of God.
18. Anybody anywhere that will not let me move forward, you will not escape the judgment of God.
19. You power that wants to stop me, my God will destroy you today in the name of Jesus Christ.
20. Father Lord, use me to break the record that no one has ever broken in the history of the world.
21. I will break the record that no one has ever broken in this nation, in the name of Jesus Christ.
22. As from today O Lord, I will be the light, I will have joy, I will shine, I will have greatness, in the name of Jesus Christ.
23. As from today O Lord, no evil will happen to me because you are in control.
24. The good things in me, the potential in me that the enemy has been suppressing, Father Lord, let it manifest now.

25. Father Lord, redirect me to focus on the right things that will make me prosper in every area and every day of my life.

LORD I BELIEVE

Passages To Read Before You Pray:
John 11:40, 5:5-9, 9:1-27, Mark 5:25-34, 9:14-29, Zechariah 4:7, Jeremiah 31:29, Ezekiel 18:1-2

PRAYER POINTS

1. O God my Father, I thank you for good things that you have begun in my life and will perfect every good work in me in the name of Jesus Christ.
2. O God my Father, I thank you for standing by your Word in my life and you will bring it to pass.
3. O God my Father, forgive me of my sins, mistakes and errors, and cleanse me in the blood of Jesus Christ.
4. I hereby cover myself in the precious blood of Jesus Christ.
5. O God my Father, open the eyes of my heart I want to see you in your glory and majesty. Reveal yourself unto me in the name of Jesus Christ.
6. O God my Father, I have brought my situation and problem to you today, pay attention to my case in the name of Jesus Christ.
7. O God my Father, as I have come before you today, my case will not be impossible.
8. O God my Father, do what no man can do in my life today and take all the glory to yourself in the name of Jesus Christ.

9. O God my Father, as I have come to your presence today, let your presence swallow my problems in the name of Jesus Christ.

10. O God my Father, let unrepentant situations in my life disappear in your presence in the name of Jesus Christ.

11. O God my Father, as I have come to your presence today, let the mountain of disappointment confronting me be removed in the name of Jesus Christ.

12. As I have come to your presence today O Lord, let the mountain of procrastination delaying my blessings be destroyed by your fire, in the name of Jesus Christ.

13. As I have come to your presence O Lord, touch my life that I will never be the same again, in the name of Jesus Christ.

14. As I have come to your presence O Lord, let the stubborn mountain of failure manifesting in my life be destroyed by the fire of God in the name of Jesus Christ.

15. As I have come to your presence O Lord, grant me the grace to experience your presence and your power, in the name of Jesus Christ.

16. It does not matter how long I have been in this situation, Father Lord, deliver me today by your power in the name of Jesus Christ.

17. It does not matter what the enemies have done in my life, Father Lord, deliver me today from the hands of the wicked in the name of Jesus Christ.

18. It does not matter if this is a generational problem; I separate myself today for a total deliverance in the name of Jesus Christ.

19. It does not matter who or what is behind my problem, I enter into God's presence today for a total deliverance in the name of Jesus Christ.

20. It does not matter how much damage this problem has done in my life, I enter into God's presence today for a total deliverance in the name of Jesus Christ.
21. Every satanic pipeline passing ancestral problems into my life, be destroyed now by the fire of God.
22. Every satanic pipeline passing generational curses into my life, be destroyed now by the fire of God, in the name of Jesus Christ.
23. Every satanic pipeline passing ancestral failure into my life, be destroyed now by the fire of God, in the name of Jesus Christ.
24. Every satanic pipeline passing generational sickness into my life, be destroyed now by the fire of God, in the name of Jesus Christ.
25. Every satanic pipeline passing ancestral poverty into my life, be destroyed by the fire of God, in the name of Jesus Christ.
26. I believe I can be successful in life, Father Lord, help my unbelief and give me what I need to be successful in everything I do in the name of Jesus Christ.
27. I believe I can breakthrough in life, Father Lord, help my unbelief and empower me to breakthrough in every area no matter the activities and the efforts of the enemy, in the name of Jesus Christ.
28. I believe I can be what you want me to be, Father Lord, help my unbelief and deliver me from every self-destructive habit, in the name of Jesus Christ.
29. I believe I can have my miracles, Father Lord, help my unbelief and let my miracles manifest now in the name of Jesus Christ.

30. I believe I can have my testimonies sooner than expected, Father Lord, help my unbelief and let my testimony come now in the name of Jesus Christ.
31. I believe I can live a better life, Father Lord, help my unbelief and let there be a turnaround in my life, in the name of Jesus Christ.
32. I believe I can make it in life, Father Lord, help my unbelief and show me the way in the name of Jesus Christ.
33. I believe I can handle and manage my promotion well, Father Lord, help my unbelief and promote me in every area in the name of Jesus Christ.
34. I believe I can handle and manage prosperity, Father Lord, help my unbelief and release financial prosperity into my life in the name of Jesus Christ.
35. I believe I can handle financial success, Father Lord, let the divine ideas flow into my life, in the name of Jesus Christ.
36. I believe I can make it to the top, Father Lord, give me the grace and strength so that I will not give up, in the name of Jesus Christ.
37. I believe I can handle and manage my breakthrough, Father Lord, help my unbelief and let my life produce great things, in the name of Jesus Christ.
38. I believe I can make it to the finish line, Father Lord, grant me the grace and strength so that I will not fall by the way side, in the name of Jesus Christ.
39. I believe I can be a blessing to my generation, Father Lord, deposit your wonders into my life, in the name of Jesus Christ.

40. I believe I can make heaven, on the basis of your mercy O Lord, help me to live a holy and sanctified life, in the name of Jesus Christ.

PURIFY ME O LORD

Passages To Read Before You Pray:
Mark 9:25-26, Job 22:27-28, Psalms 24, 1, 15, 99

PRAYER POINTS

1. O God my Father, I thank you for your Word is yes and amen, and your Word will surely come to pass in my life.
2. O God my Father, I thank you for the good things that you have started in my life and you will perfect it in the name of Jesus Christ.
3. O God my Father, I thank you for always being there for me and with me in the name of Jesus Christ.
4. O God my Father, when I find myself in the time of trouble, when all hope is lost, thank you for being there for me.
5. Father Lord, on the basis of your mercy, forgive me of all my sins and cleanse me in the blood of Jesus Christ.
6. You spirit of spiritual laziness, I command you to get out of my life and come back no more in the name of Jesus Christ.
7. You spirit of spiritual slumber, I command you to get out of my life and come back no more in the name of Jesus Christ.
8. You spirit of rebellion, I command you to get out of my life and come back no more, in the name of Jesus Christ.
9. You spirit of anger, I command you to get out of my life and come back no more in the name of Jesus Christ.

10. You spirit of pride, I command you to get out of my life and come back no more, in the name of Jesus Christ.
11. You spirit of spiritual adultery, I command you to get out of my life and come back no more, in the name of Jesus Christ.
12. You spirit of ignorance, I command you to get out of my life and come back no more, in the name of Jesus Christ.
13. You spirit of hatred, I command you to get out of my life and come back no more, in the name of Jesus Christ.
14. You spirit of selfishness, I command you to get out of my life and come back no more, in the name of Jesus Christ.
15. You spirit of self-righteousness, I command you to get out of my life and come back no more, in the name of Jesus Christ.
16. You spirit of greediness, I command you to get out of my life and come back no more, in the name of Jesus Christ.
17. You spirit of jealousy, I command you to get out of my life and come back no more, in the name of Jesus Christ.
18. You spirit of impurity, I command you to get out of my life and come back no more, in the name of Jesus Christ.
19. You spirit of addiction, I command you to get out of my life and come back no more, in the name of Jesus Christ.
20. You spirit of sexual immorality, I command you to get out of my life and come back no more, in the name of Jesus Christ.
21. You spirit of unbelief, I command you to get out of my life and come back no more, in the name of Jesus Christ.
22. You spirit of doubt, I command you to get out of my life and come back no more, in the name of Jesus Christ.

23. You lying spirit, I command you to get out of life and come back no more, in the name of Jesus Christ.
24. You spirit of division, I command you to get out of my life and come back no more, in the name of Jesus Christ.
25. You spirit of sinful desire, I command you to get out of my life and come back no more, in the name of Jesus Christ.
26. You spirit of idolatry, I command you to get out of my life and come back no more, in the name of Jesus Christ.
27. You spirit of confusion, I command you to get out of my life and come back no more, in the name of Jesus Christ.
28. You spirit of fear, I command you to get out of my life and come back no more, in the name of Jesus Christ.
29. You spirit of disobedience, I command you to get out of my life and come back no more, in the name of Jesus Christ.
30. You spirit of spiritual blindness, I command you to get out of my life and come back no more, in the name of Jesus Christ.
31. You spirit of prayerlessness, I command you to get out of my life and come back no more, in the name of Jesus Christ.
32. You spirit of spiritual deafness, I command you to get out of my life and come back no more, in the name of Jesus Christ.
33. You spirit of spiritual dumbness, I command you to get out of my life and come back no more, in the name of Jesus Christ.
34. You spirit of timidity, I command you to get out of my life and come back no more, in the name of Jesus Christ.

35. You spirit of self-justification, I command you to get out of my life and come back no more, in the name of Jesus Christ.

36. You manipulating spirit, I command you to get out of my life and come back no more, in the name of Jesus Christ.

37. You spirit of deception, I command you to get out of my life and come back no more, in the name of Jesus Christ.

38. You spirit of lawlessness, I command you to get out of my life and come back no more, in the name of Jesus Christ.

39. You spirit of self-exaltation I command you to get out of my life and come back no more, in the name of Jesus Christ.

40. You sprit of stubbornness, I command you to. Get out of my life and come back no more, in the name of Jesus Christ.

41. You spirit of spiritual slavery, I command you to get out of my life and come back no more, in the name of Jesus Christ.

42. You spirit of lust, I command you to get out of my life and come back no more, in the name of Jesus Christ.

43. You spirit of false doctrine, I command you to get out of my life and come back no more, in the name of Jesus Christ.

44. You spirit of malice, I command you to get out of my life and come back no more, in the name of Jesus Christ.

45. You spirit of hopelessness, I command you to get out of my life and come back no more, in the name of Jesus Christ.

46. You spirit of bitterness, I command you to get out of my life and come back no more, in the name of Jesus Christ.

47. You spirit of evil speaking, I command you to get out of my life and come back no more, in the name of Jesus Christ.
48. You spirit of impatience, I command you to get out of my life and come back no more, in the name of Jesus Christ.
49. You spirit self-condemnation, I command you to get out of my life and come back no more, in the name of Jesus Christ.
50. You spirit of worldliness, I command you to get out of my life and come back no more, in the name of Jesus Christ.
51. You spirit of indecision, I command you to get out of my life and come back no more, in the name of Jesus Christ.
52. You spirit of double-mindedness, I command you to get out of my life and come back no more, in the name of Jesus Christ.
53. You spirit of false profession, I command you to get out of my life and come back no more, in the name of Jesus Christ.
54. You spirit of inconsistency, I command you to get out of my life and come back no more, in the name of Jesus Christ.
55. You spirit of spiritual instability, I command you to get out of my life and come back no more, in the name of Jesus Christ.

I SHALL SEE IT AGAIN NO MORE

Passages To Read Before You Pray:
Exodus 3:7-10, 14:13-18, John 11:44, Psalms 35, 18, 69

PRAYER POINTS

1. O God my Father, I thank you for all that you are doing in my life.
2. O God my Father, I thank you for always being there for me.
3. O God my Father, I thank you for your grace and mercy that I receive day after day.
4. On the basis of your mercy O Lord, forgive me of my sins and errors, and cleanse me in the precious blood of Jesus Christ.
5. Today O Lord, reveal yourself unto me the way I have never seen you before in the name of Jesus Christ.
6. I refuse to pray in vain, my prayers will produce the desired results in the name of Jesus Christ.
7. Today O Lord, demonstrate your power in every area of my life, in the name of Jesus Christ.
8. O God my Father, send my Moses today to deliver me from any form of slavery, in the name of Jesus Christ.
9. O God my Father send my Moses today to deliver me from any form of bondage in the name of Jesus Christ.
10. O God my Father, send my Moses today to deliver me from any form of captivity, in the name of Jesus Christ.
11. O God my Father, send my Moses today to deliver me from any form of affliction, in the name of Jesus Christ.

12. Affliction will not happen the second time in my life in the name of Jesus Christ.
13. O God my Father, send my Moses today to deliver me from the hands of the taskmasters, in the name of Jesus Christ.
14. O God my Father, send my Moses today to deliver me from the hands of the oppressors, in the name of Jesus Christ.
15. Hear my cry today O Lord, and deliver me from sorrows.
16. Hear my cry today O Lord, and deliver me from hopelessness, in the name of Jesus Christ.
17. Hear my cry today O Lord, and deliver me from every long time problem manifesting in life, in the name of Jesus Christ.
18. O God my Father, bring me out of every stubborn situation by your power in the name of Jesus Christ.
19. You power of the grave contending with my glory, loose me and let me go, in the name of Jesus Christ.
20. You power of failure that is holding my life back, loose me and let me go, in the name of Jesus Christ.
21. You spirit of stagnancy that refuses to let me move forward, loose me and let me go in the name of Jesus Christ.
22. You spirit of unbelief that is robbing me of my blessings, loose me and let me go in the name of Jesus Christ.
23. All inherited curses manifesting in my life, your time is up, loose me and let me go in the name of Jesus Christ.
24. Every curse of financial embarrassment manifesting in my life, loose me and let me go in the name of Jesus Christ.

25. You spirit of confusion assigned against me, loose me and let me go in the name of Jesus Christ.
26. You spirit of retrogression assigned to make my life go backward, loose me and let me go in the name of Jesus Christ.
27. You spirit of infirmity assigned to torment me, loose me and let me go in the name of Jesus Christ.
28. You spirit of poverty manifesting in my life, loose me and let me go in the name of Jesus Christ.
29. You spirit of loneliness assigned against me, loose me and let me go in the name of Jesus Christ.
30. I believe with all my heart, the problems that I see in my life today, I shall see it again no more, in the name of Jesus Christ.
31. I believe with all my heart that failure manifesting in my life today, I shall see no more in the name of Jesus Christ.
32. I believe with all my heart, stagnancy that is manifesting in my life today; I shall see it again no more in the name of Jesus Christ.
33. I believe with all my heart, financial embarrassment that is manifesting in my life today, I shall see it again no more in the name of Jesus Christ.
34. I believe with all my heart, barrenness that is manifesting in my life today, I shall see it again no more in the name of Jesus Christ.
35. I believe with all my heart, the oppressors that are oppressing me today, I shall see it again no more in the name of Jesus Christ.
36. I believe with all my heart, household wickedness that is troubling me today, I shall see it again no more in the name of Jesus Christ.

37. I believe with all my heart, satanic embargo that is placed on my life today, I shall see it again no more in the name of Jesus Christ.
38. I believe with all my heart, every burden upon my shoulder today, I shall see it again no more in the name of Jesus Christ.
39. I believe with all my heart, every yoke upon my neck today, I shall see it again no more in the name of Jesus Christ.
40. Every power assigned to make my life miserable, I shall see it again no more in the name of Jesus Christ.
41. Every power assigned to hinder my prayers, I shall see it again no more in the name of Jesus Christ.
42. Every power assigned to hinder my miracles, I shall see it again no more in the name of Jesus Christ.
43. Every power assigned to block my breakthrough, I shall see it again no more in the name of Jesus Christ.
44. Every power assigned to kill my dreams, I shall it again no more in the name of Jesus Christ.
45. Every power assigned to torment me, I shall see it again no more in the name of Jesus Christ.
46. Every power that is working against my success, I shall see it again no more in the name of Jesus Christ.
47. Every power that is working against my prosperity, I shall see it again no more in the name of Jesus Christ.
48. Every power that is attacking my marriage, I shall see it again no more in the name of Jesus Christ.
49. Every power assigned to rob me of my joy, I shall see it again no more in the name of Jesus Christ.

THIS IS MY TIME

Passages To Read Before You Pray:
Habakkuk 2: 2-3, Isaiah 41: 10-13, Psalms 27, Matthew 7:7-11,
John 11:40

PRAYER POINTS

1. O God my Father, I thank you for your Word is yes and amen, and your Word will surely come to pass in my life.
2. O God my Father, I thank you for the good things that you have started in my life and you will perfect it in the name of Jesus Christ.
3. O God my Father, I thank you for always being there for me and with me in the name of Jesus Christ.
4. O God my Father, when I find myself in the time of trouble, when all hope is lost, thank you for being there for me.
5. Father Lord, on the basis of your mercy, forgive me of all my sins and cleanse me in the blood of Jesus Christ.
6. By your grace and mercy O Lord, I will not pray in vain.
7. As I cry O Lord, let my prayers produce desired results.
8. O God my Father, grant me the grace to have a clear understanding of your plans for my life.
9. O God my Father, open my eyes to see what you have in place for me.
10. O God my Father, open my eyes of understanding to know what I am supposed to do with my life.
11. O God my Father, direct my path and lead me to where you want me to be to fulfill my God-given purpose.

12. Fear will not stop me from taking the step of faith that lead to my promotion.
13. Fear will not stop me from taking the step of faith that lead to my breakthroughs.
14. Fear will not stop me from taking action that will lead to my financial freedom.
15. Fear will not stop me from taking action that will lead to my total deliverance.
16. Fear will not stop me from waiting on the Lord.
17. O God my Father, grant me the grace to work in agreement with your plans concerning my life.
18. I will not work against the plan of God for my life.
19. This year shall be my appointed year, the year of my promotion.
20. This year shall be my appointed year, the year of my financial freedom.
21. This year shall be my appointed year, the year of my uncommon breakthrough in the name of Jesus Christ.
22. This year shall be my appointed year, the year of my revelation in the name of Jesus Christ.
23. This year shall be my appointed year, the year of my outstanding success in the name of Jesus Christ.
24. This year shall be my appointed year, the year of my unstoppable progress in the name of Jesus Christ.
25. This year shall be my appointed year, the year of my dumbfounding testimonies in the nam elf Jesus Christ.
26. This year shall be my appointed year, the year of my great celebration in the name of Jesus Christ.
27. This year shall be my appointed year, the year of my unending harvest in the name of Jesus Christ.

28. This year shall be my appointed year, the year of new things in every area of my life in the name of Jesus Christ.
29. This year shall be my appointed year, the year of my open heaven in the name of Jesus Christ.
30. This year shall be my appointed year, the year of restoration in the name of Jesus Christ.
31. This year shall be my appointed year, the year of my great achievement in the name of Jesus Christ.
32. This year shall be my appointed year, the year of the fulfillment of God's promises in my life I the name of Jesus Christ.
33. This year, my testimonies will surely come without any delay in the name of Jesus Christ.
34. This year, my promotion will surely come without any delay in the name of Jesus Christ.
35. This year, my blessing will surely come without any delay in the name of Jesus Christ.
36. This year, my financial freedom will surely come without any delay in the name of Jesus Christ.
37. This year, my breakthrough will surely come without any delay in the name of Jesus Christ.
38. This year, I will have outstanding success in my life without any delay or hindrance in the name of Jesus Christ.
39. This year, I will experience unstoppable progress in my life without any hindrance or delay in the name of Jesus Christ.
40. This year, my testimony will come without any hindrance or delay it he name of Jesus Christ.

41. This year, there will be celebration in my life, home, business, ministry and every area of my interest in the name of Jesus Christ.
42. This year, my harvest will come without any hindrance or delay, and my harvest will be plenteous in the name of Jesus Christ.
43. This year, my greatest achievement so far will surely come without any hindrance, delay or limitation in the name of Jesus Christ.
44. From the beginning to the end of this year, I will enjoy new things in every area of my life, in the name of Jesus Christ.
45. From the beginning to the end of this year, my heaven shall continually open without any delay or limitation in the name of Jesus Christ.

THE MEANING OF DELIVERANCE

IS MY SITUATION NORMAL?

1. Deliverance means to loose the bounds of wickedness.
    A lot of people are under the bondage of wickedness. If
    you look at the lives of many people, you will discover a
    wide array of wicked occurrences. If your life is
    surrounded by wicked mysterious happenings, you need
    to go for deliverance as fast as you can.

2. Deliverance centers on the destruction of the yoke of the
    enemy.
    A yoke is anything that hinders or sets you back.
    Whatever sets you back from moving forward in your
    life is a yoke. God's will is that you move forward and
    attain divine goals set for your life. When the contrary
    happens, there is a bondage hanging above your life.

3. Deliverance is to break curses and evil covenants.
    The ancestors of many people were cursed and the
    curses have flown down the family line. For example, if
    a person struggles without any tangible achievement in
    life, there is a problem somewhere.

4. Deliverance is the spiritual cleansing of an environment.
    Some people bought or built houses on land that were
    once cursed; or live in an apartment building with a co-
    tenant that is under curses and their lives and family are
    affected. Unless deliverance is conducted on such
    persons or families, things will remain negative.

5. Deliverance is the breaking of satanic chain that has made fruitfulness or prosperity impossible for people. There is an invisible chain which has acted as a stubborn barrier between you and your success. A lot of people have tried their possible best for prosperity but nothing has been experienced that can be termed real prosperity.

6. Deliverance is the removal of invisible loads laid on people.
   What many people carry goes beyond just burdens of life. Men and women bear burdens that are laid on their backs by the kingdom of darkness. When such a burden becomes too heavy (it will always be) people will always be forced to act irrationally.

7. Deliverance is uprooting evil seeds from people's lives. Unknown to many people, evil seeds would have been consumed in the days of ignorance. Such seeds often grow into invisible evil trees in the lives of many people. How can someone succeed in life, when an evil tree is in his or her life?

8. Deliverance is the removal of satanic embargo.
   In many instances, some people struggle with unseen embargoes. No matter how hardworking you are, you will be working like an elephant but eating like a rat. Success becomes a tale in the life of such a person. One single embargo in your life can keep you in satanic slavery forever.

9. Deliverance is the release from the power of darkness.

Many people are under the bondage of powers of darkness and they don't know. They are not free to move towards the divine direction. Instead of going forward, they keep going backward. There is every indication that satanic powers have kept them under bondage. It takes deliverance to set you free. Don't wait another day take a step today.

10. Deliverance is being set free from compulsive evil habits and actions.
There are some people who knowingly or unknowingly often misbehave and cause problems repeatedly in their own lives. If you fall into this group, you need to undergo deliverance.

11. Deliverance is being set free from habits that enslave.
Many people struggle with enslaving habits secretly. Deliverance is the answer.

12. Deliverance is freedom from stubborn hindrances to spiritual growth.
A lot of people (even minister) find it difficult to make necessary spiritual progress. Many people have struggled for years in order to be baptized with the Holy Ghost without success. Of course, demonic bondage will make such spiritual experiences difficult to attain.

13. Deliverance involves being completely set free from past occult bondage.
A good number of so-called children of God are yet to experience total deliverance from the occult. This kind

of deliverance is needed for those who have gone very far with the devil.

14. Deliverance is being set free from chronic sinful habits.
If you are involved one way or the other in any sinful habit whatsoever or any addiction, you need serious deliverance.

15. Deliverance includes being set free from sickness that defies medical diagnosis.
If you have tried every possibility medically speaking because of sickness and efforts towards getting the best medical help but it has yielded no result, you need serious deliverance. Jesus is the greatest doctor I know, He can and will heal you.

16. Deliverance means being set free from restlessness, mental confusion and other malignant problems.
As a child of God, you must not struggle with restlessness, mind blankness and memory failure. If you have experienced such conditions, you need deliverance. Don't wait another day.

17. Deliverance is being set free from inexplicable family break ups (divorce) and recurrent squabbles in the family.
You were raised by a single parent; and you also end up being a single parent; you have being divorced or going through divorce, you have many children with different fathers, there are demonic activities in your home. When your marriage is suffering attacks from the spirit called "Home Destroyer". When your spouse is avoiding

his/her responsibilities in marriage/home, you need serious deliverance. Don't wait another day, seek and get deliverance today.

18. Deliverance is being set free from the binding power of an evil trend of recurrent family troubles and tragedy. When you count two or three people in your family that have ended up in prison, or suffered from drug addiction, or untimely death, or unexplainable sickness, or rebellious children, or poverty flow in your bloodline, or failure at the edge of breakthrough; you need serious deliverance, run without delay and seek deliverance.

19. Deliverance is being set free from mysterious spiritual experiences.
If you go through normal channels of prayers, spiritual discipline and application of the Word of God, yet victory is elusive, you need deliverance.

20. You need to cry unto God for deliverance today. If you have spent your life journey in the wilderness, you need to run to God as fast as your feet can carry you. If you are contemplating quitting this battle of life (suicide), you must go for deliverance as soon as possible.

21. If you have concluded that you have had more than a fair share of life's problems, you need to visit the deliverance clinic as soon as possible.

22. If bad luck has continued to trail your life in spite of the fact that you are a child of God, you need deliverance. If you have discovered that the same kind of bondage that

is found in the life of any member of your immediate and extended family is visibly present in your life; don't wait another day, go for deliverance today.

Other books written by Tim Atunnise:

- Prayer of The Day – Volume I

- Prayer of The Day – Volume II

- Prayer of The Day – Volume III

- Prayer of The Day – Volume IV

- Overcoming Self (Sunday School Manual)

- Overcoming Self (Teacher's Copy)

- The Parables (Sunday School Manual)

- The Parables (Teacher's Copy)

- The Fruit of the Spirit (Sunday School Manual)

- The Fruit of the Spirit (Teacher's Copy)

- The Book of Daniel Made Easy

- The Miracles of Jesus Christ (Sunday School Manual)

- Divine Prescriptions

- I Must Win This Battle (Personal Deliverance)

- Lost & Found: The House of Israel

- The Book of Exodus (Bible Study Manual)

Notes

19383775R00119

Made in the USA
Charleston, SC
21 May 2013